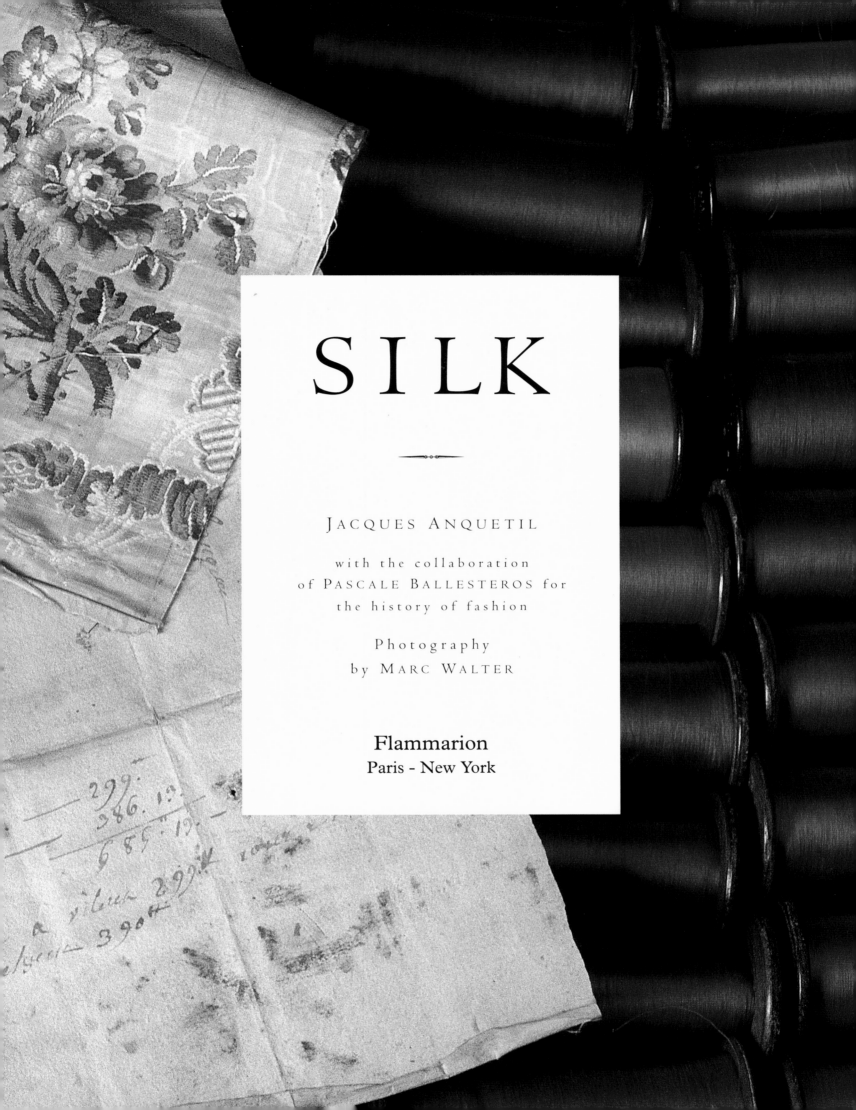

SILK

—◆—

JACQUES ANQUETIL

with the collaboration
of PASCALE BALLESTEROS for
the history of fashion

Photography
by MARC WALTER

Flammarion
Paris - New York

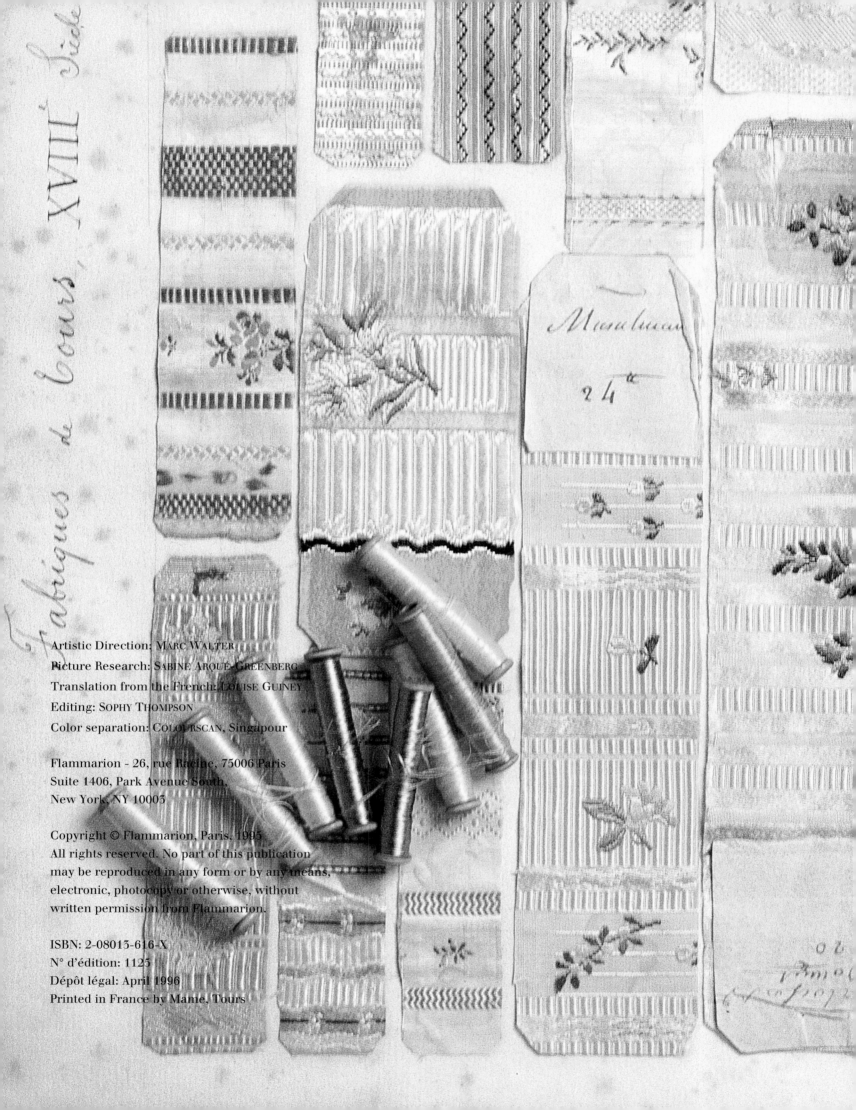

Fabriques de tours, XVIIIᵉ Siècle

Artistic Direction: MARC WALTER
Picture Research: SABINE ARQUÉ-GREENBERG
Translation from the French: LOUISE GUINEY
Editing: SOPHY THOMPSON
Color separation: COLOURSCAN, Singapour

Flammarion - 26, rue Racine, 75006 Paris
Suite 1406, Park Avenue South,
New York, NY 10003

ISBN: 2-08013-616-X
N° d'édition: 1125
Dépôt légal: April 1996
Printed in France by Mame, Tours

Contents

INTRODUCTION

Previous pages:

Order book. Nineteenth century.

Samples. Eighteenth century.

Jean Roze archives, Tours.

Most of the silk fabrics we present in this work have a symbolic and emotional value far surpassing the merely utilitarian. Silk touches on the realm of the invisible, the sacred. The special magic of silk stems from its interaction with light, which it refracts in a way similar to objects found in nature, such as the minuscule scales on a butterfly's wings or the iridescent mother-of-pearl interiors of sea shells. Long before it is woven into cloth, silk is subjected to complex processing in order to preserve this luminous quality, this shimmer and brilliance. When light plays on a piece of silk, the weave appears, in turn, to glisten, glitter, change color, become moiré, lustrous, or matte. Silk is capable of such infinite metamorphosis that no adjective can ever describe it exactly.

Silk fabrics are mirrors of all the civilizations in which they have played a part. They are records of the vast migrations that human beings have embarked upon over the centuries, taking with them their philosophies, technological discoveries, artistic designs, and religious symbols. Every piece of silk, from fragments discovered in tombs along the Silk Road to the most sophisticated contemporary creation from Lyon or Italy, bears traces of the many cultures, myths and legends of the past. In the folds of figured silk lie the imprint of their distant oriental origins, as well as the timeless motifs which artists have maintained, expressing them in each generation to reflect contemporary idioms. Silk appeals to the deepest instincts of the imagination, confirming as no other material could the truth of Gaston Bachelard's assertion that "One has never seen the world well if he has not dreamed what he was seeing."

The following pages reveal that throughout history the universal language of silk—its motifs and symbols—may almost be described as a system of writing, a fact underlined by the technical terminology: the artisan in Lyon, Tours, Venice, or Florence who punches the holes for silk designs onto dobby cards for Jacquard looms is called a "reader," and the task itself "reading" in or off.

Silk brocade being woven on a Jacquard loom using small bobbin shuttles. Prelle, Lyon.

Left:

Handwoven imitation Genoa velvet on a Jacquard loom.

Trois Tours factory.

Le Manach, Tours.

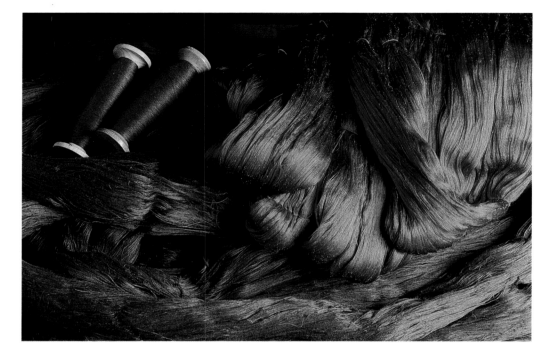

Our own era is rich in paradox. Contemporary high-tech automated looms cannot reproduce certain types of complicated upholstery silk and brocade once woven on now antiquated Jacquard looms. However, a number of major weavers located in cities along the old silk routes have succeeded in restoring the antique looms, thus contributing to the preservation of a priceless artisanal heritage. These firms are the only ones able to reproduce the sumptuous embroidered silks and luxurious gold and silver brocades used in refurbishing the restored interiors of French châteaux such as Versailles, Fontainebleau, Saint-Cloud, and Compiègne.

I remember my first visit, in 1977, to the Prelle workrooms, where I met Pierre Rocher, an old-time *canut* (Lyon silk weaver), sadly no longer alive today. At the time of my visit, Rocher was working on a magnificent silk brocade threaded with silver and gold for the king's bedchamber at Versailles, but his output was only two to three inches per day. He recalled with nostalgia how "Less than twenty years ago you could hear the constant clatter of looms on every single floor of this building." Today, thanks to the determination and vision of François Verzier, current heir to the family firm in Lyon's Croix-Rousse district, Rocher's work is being continued by a team of old-timers like himself, both men and women. As Verzier explains, "Traditional Lyon handweaving must be preserved. Our company, like Tassinari, is a living museum." The story of the principal French and Italian firms that have con-

tributed so much to maintaining the venerable silk-weaving tradition for both upholstery and clothing fabrics is recounted in the following pages.

Although silk production has been revolutionized by modern science and technology, its original values have remained intact. These are the same values on which all great art is based: to express, through realistic or abstract images (which in this case can be woven, printed, dyed, or embroidered as well as painted), the conception of the world held by a particular civilization at a particular moment in its history and thus to produce a unique mirror reflecting humankind's joy, sorrow, hope, fear, and a love of the natural world—from the illustrations of flora and fauna so ably executed by designer Philippe de Lasalle in the eighteenth century, to Raoul Dufy's playful animal designs in the twentieth. Silk is a material that provides its artists—whether weavers, embroiderers, or specialists in trimming and ribbon work—with a medium in which they can express themselves fully through color and texture. Artists who work with silk are colorists and sculptors in fabric. This is particularly well-illustrated in the case of ciselé velvet, for example, executed by artisans using only a plain stylus to shear the delicate threads in a piece of satin until the *velours sabres* effect so prized by the greatest couturiers is achieved.

Textile art as applied to fashion occupies a large portion of the present work. Here we learn that, over the centuries, the design of silk clothing has required even greater aesthetic vision and sensitivity of perception than the design of silk upholstery. This is because the pattern, cut, and volume of a silk garment—whether worn by a man or a woman—will condition the way its colors shimmer and shift in response to light and movement. For example, the optical effect characteristic of

Seal used to stamp approved fabrics. Tours, 1786. Archives départementales, Indre-et-Loire.

pour les Etoffes reglées

marque, et fibres.

Right:

Jacquard loom. Each warp thread moves independently in response the pattern on a perforated card. The top of the loom is called the overhead board. Trois Tours factory. Le Manach, Tours.

Shelves of sample silks.
Tassinari et Chatel
salesroom, Paris.

chameleon taffeta, which changes color depending on the angle of vision and the light, is produced by combining a satin with a taffeta weave.

Silk-weaving techniques evolved in response to underlying structural laws which govern, for example, the way in which a garment hangs, or ensure that a series of pleats perfectly reflects the contrast between light and shadow. This is borne out by the meticulous care with which the great painters of the Italian Renaissance rendered the silks worn by their subjects, and by the Flemish masters' depictions of light reflected on silk garments, especially in their paintings of the Virgin Mary.

Yet silk is not just a feast for the eyes, it is also a pleasure for the more subtle sense of touch, which Marc Walter's photographs have made almost tangible. Our skin thrills to the caress of silk taffeta, the soft touch of satin and velvet. Throughout history, silk in all of its guises has always had a mysterious life of its own.

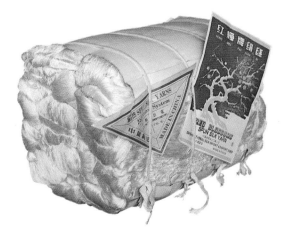

Five-kilo (eleven-pound) bale of Chinese silk with original label. Methods for baling and wrapping have changed little since the days of the Silk Road.

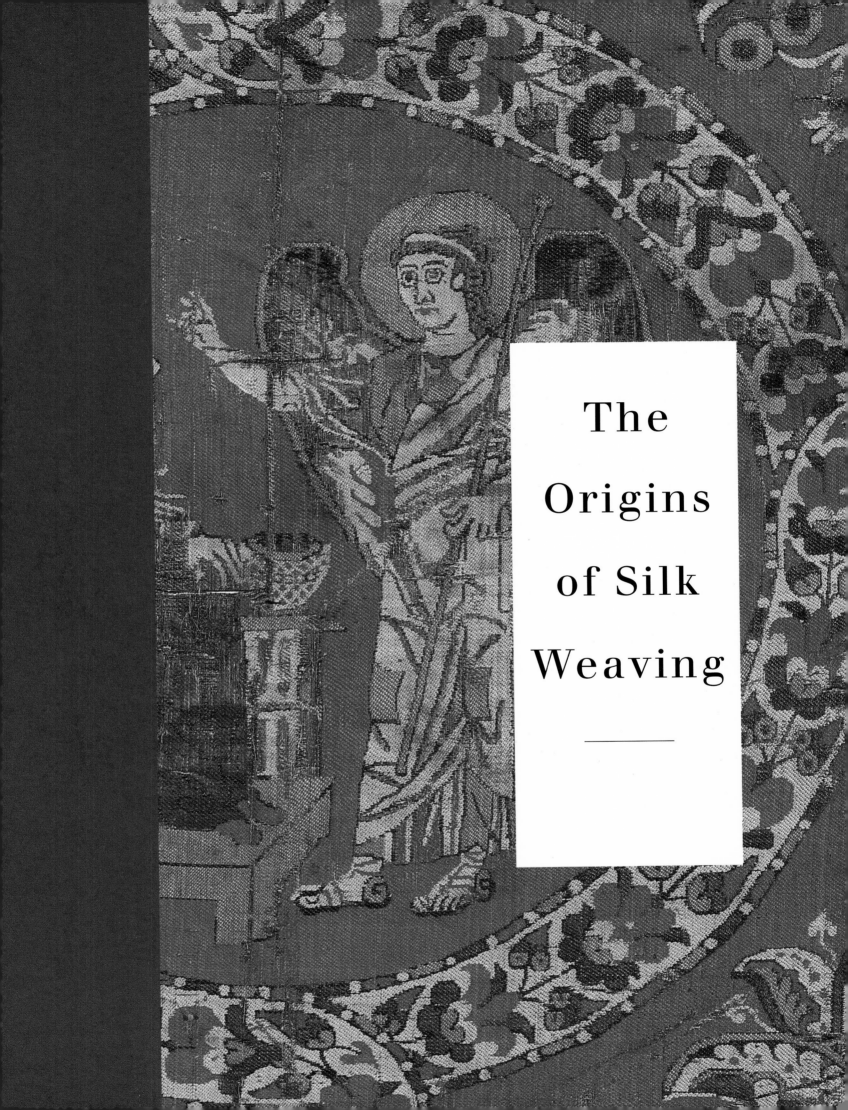

The Origins of Silk Weaving

CHINA DISCOVERS SERICULTURE

In his book of *Odes*, Confucius recounts the legendary discovery of silk by the Chinese Princess Hsi-Ling, wife of Emperor Huang-Ti (*circa* 2700 B.C.). The princess was drinking tea under a mulberry tree one day, when a cocoon fell into her cup. "She started to play with the tiny gray ball, and was amazed to find it contained a delicate thread of extraordinary texture." According to Chinese tradition, sericulture began with Princess Hsi-Ling, but more reliable evidence suggests that systematic silkworm breeding did not truly get underway until several centuries later. Bone carvings from the Shang dynasty (*circa* 1500–1050 B.C.) bear ideograms denoting "silk thread," "mulberry tree," and "bombyx" (silkworm moth), and cocoon-shaped amulets have been excavated from an ancient Chinese tomb. Bronzes dating from the same period carry the imprint of the fabrics in which they were once wrapped, transferred by oxidation as the material decomposed. These diamond-shaped patterns prove the existence of a technically advanced silk-weaving industry at the time.

The first cocoons used for making silk were almost certainly in their natural state. However, the filament from wild cocoons cannot be reeled, since the moth uses an acid secretion to pierce the cocoon, severing the long silk filament into thousands of smaller pieces which then have to be carded and spun like cotton or wool. The stroke of genius that transformed this primitive silk-weaving process—and gave the Chinese their unique monopoly—was the realization that if the silkworm is bred in captivity and the chrysalis killed before it can pierce the cocoon, the long filament will remain unbroken. The secret of silkworm breeding, and the commercial monopoly to which it gave rise, was jealousy guarded by the Chinese over many centuries. Frontier controls were strict. Travelers leaving China—pilgrims, merchants, and high government officials alike—were all searched at the border. Would-be smugglers unfortunate enough to be discovered harboring silkworm eggs or mulberry-tree seeds in their luggage were decapitated on the spot.

Chinese Sericulture

The caterpillar of the *Bombyx mori,* the silkworm moth, feeds only on the leaves of the white mulberry tree. Silkworm breeding therefore depends on a highly developed agricultural system capable of sustaining the large-scale cultivation of mulberry trees. Furthermore, harvesting the fresh leaves is a labor-intensive task. Silkworm breeding is a difficult and risky enterprise; when it was a cottage industry people erected temples to the silk goddess in their homes to ensure a fruitful harvest. The silkworm larvae, called silk seed, are reared on bamboo trays and fed a steady diet of mulberry leaves day and night for about six weeks. As the larvae increase in size, they outgrow their skins and molt. By the fourth molting they will have grown to a little over three inches in length. At this point the silkworms are removed from the feeding trays and placed on tiers of shelves covered with straw or a similar material to which they can attach their cocoons. The larvae settle onto individual stalks, and over the space of four days they completely surround themselves with a viscous secretion emitted in a single strand. This substance, which hardens on contact with the air, is the silk filament.

When the cocoons are completed, the larvae inside begin their metamorphosis into chrysalises. At this stage, the cocoons are sorted. Defective cocoons are carded and spun immediately, and a certain number of perfect cocoons are set aside for reproductive purposes. When the cocoons have been sorted, the final harvest can be estimated. Approximately twelve pounds of cocoons are needed to make one pound of raw silk.

After sorting, the cocoons are placed on new trays in a temperature-controlled room. Just before their final metamorphosis, the chrysalises are killed by suffocation to prevent them from piercing the cocoons, which are then dipped in a bath of scalding water to soften the filaments and make them easier to reel. Since the filament from a single cocoon would not be strong enough to withstand the rigors of weaving, four to six filaments are twisted together before being run through a tracking eyelet and reeled onto a bamboo rod. On contact with the air, the separate filaments solidify into a single thread. After the raw silk has been reeled, it is wound into separate skeins for dyeing. In ancient China, solid-color and small-patterned silks were woven on pedal looms, and those with more complex patterns on draw-looms. Weavers sold their silks to private customers, reserving their highest-quality cloth for the local tailors who supplied members of the imperial court with magnificent robes. One type of silk fabric, shantung, which is still produced in China today from the cocoons of either *Bombyx mori* or other wild silkworm moths, derives its name from the region where it is woven (Shandong).

Harvesting mulberry leaves.

Unhatched cocoons.

Scalding the cocoons prior to reeling.

PIONEERS OF THE SILK ROAD

By the reign of Cyrus, king of Persia (558?–529 B.C.), the Achaemenids had established themselves as rulers over western Asia. Their empire stretched from the Mediterranean Sea to India, and encroached ever nearer to China. A contemporary 350-foot frieze, still visible under the terrace of the great council chamber at Persepolis, in the mountains of Iran, depicts emissaries from throughout the empire paying tribute to Xerxes I (486?–465 B.C.), a subsequent Persian ruler. The faces and native dress of each emissary have been rendered in meticulous detail by the Persian sculptors. The frieze shows envoys from Media, Khuzistan, Herat, Egypt, Parthia, Sogdiana, Babylonia, Cilicia, and India, as well as representatives sent by the Scythian nomads and Arabian Bedouins. Depicted among the emissaries' offerings are the Bactrian camels and Syrian dromedaries that were later used to transport silk from China.

The Persian Empire erased old borders. Suddenly goods, people, and ideas could travel freely over long distances. The roads built to link this vast empire together proved crucial to the success of Alexander the Great's campaigns of conquest, and they also opened the way for the caravans that, two centuries later, were to carry raw and woven Chinese silks to Antioch and Alexandria.

Alexander the Great

Like Cyrus before him, Alexander of Macedonia attempted to fuse all the peoples of Central Asia into a single Greco-Persian melting-pot. The major trading centers along the Silk Road came into being as a result of Alexander's insatiable thirst for conquest. New cities sprang up in his wake, and the roads built between them linked distant civilizations. When Alexander died in Babylon in 323 B.C., a cult developed around his memory, venerating him as "Iskander," or in Islamic countries "Dul-Qarnaïn" (two-horned). It was at this point that history and legend became intertwined, and Muslims began to worship Alexander as a divine messenger sent by God to defend the faith.

General Zhang Qian

It was by order of the Western Han emperor Wudi (140–87 B.C.) that General Zhang Qian was sent as envoy to establish diplomatic contacts between China and "the countries of the West" in order to protect the roads of Central Asia against incessant attacks by Xiongnu nomads. Zhang Qian was away from home for ten adventure-filled years. Although he failed in his peace mission, the reports he brought back describing the countries he had seen were instrumental in the Chinese emperor's decision to open up cultural and trade exchanges, primarily with the Parthians. This period marks the beginning of the Silk Road. In A.D. 97, Chinese General Ban Shao won control of the Tarim Basin, securing an overland caravan route extending as far as Khotan. The period of this *pax sinica* was a golden age for the Sino-Parthian silk trade. The oasis cities dotted along the Silk Road became focal points of contact between the religions and philosophies of East and West, immortalized first in the decorative motifs on Chinese, Persian and, later on, Byzantine silks.

Silk Trade between Han Dynasty China, Parthia, and Rome

In order to satisfy their taste for luxury, the Parthian rulers expanded trade relations with the West, most notably with their arch-enemies the Romans, who by 65 B.C. had annexed Syria and controlled the vast majority of the land and sea trade routes in the Middle East.

Chinese silk was, it would seem, first discovered by the Romans during the battle of Carrhae in 53 B.C. At a critical point in the battle, the Parthian cavalry unfurled huge multicolored silk banners before the wondering eyes of Crassus's troops. The Romans ordered their spies to find out more about these banners, which they learned came from distant "silk peoples," the Seres, who traded with the Parthians over a mysterious route. However, silk fabric did not become common in Rome until the reign of Augustus (27–14 B.C.), by which time there were so many middlemen between Chang'an and Rome that a pound of silk was literally worth its weight in gold.

Persepolis frieze. Sixth to fifth century B.C. Detail showing a Bactrian camel offered to the king of Persia.

Coptic tapestry showing Alexander the Great being crowned as a Christian saint.

Fresco in the Dunhuang caves (Gansu province, China) showing merchants being robbed by bandits. Seventh to ninth century.

Coptic tapestry discovered by archaeologists at Antinopolis showing the king of Persia seated on his throne, observing a battle between horsemen executing the backwards "Parthian" shot.

Miniature from Firdausi's *Book of Kings*.

The Emperor Ghazan in front of his tent.
History of the Mongols, by Rashid ed-Din, Herat.

SASSANID PERSIA AND BYZANTIUM

Sassanid Traders Gain Control over the Silk Road

Under the Sassanid dynasty, Persia became the hub of all existing civilizations, old and new. The Persian empire owed its pivotal position between East and West to its location (midway between Byzantium, China, and India), its size, its military power, and its cultural influence. Because the Sassanids controlled so many of the routes over which silk was transported, the empire soon monopolized the Chinese silk trade. The two great contemporary silk centers, Constantinople and Ctesiphon, were described by travelers who visited them as the "eyes of the world." The innate love of eastern peoples for bright colors was amply served by the vivid and contrasting hues of contemporary textiles and mosaic tiles. Sumptuous carpets covered the floors, and many silks were further enhanced with gleaming threads of gold and silver.

Byzantine "Mozac" silk, named after the Abbaye de Mozac. Eighth century.

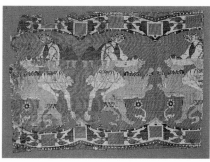

Silver platter showing King Peroz I (A.D. 459–584) hunting.

The classic Sassanid hunting-scene motif was imitated by Byzantine and Chinese weavers, who transmitted it to Japan via Korea. These royal hunt scenes, which are found on silks, carpets, and on flat silverware, were more than mere illustrations of a sovereign's leisure pursuits; they were symbolic expressions of his divinity. The king is always shown crowned, richly attired, and mounted on horseback. He aims his arrows over his left shoulder in what is known as the "Parthian" shot. Every aspect of the image is stylized: the crown, the fluttering ribbons, and the hieratic attitudes of the sacred animals. These images also served as a type of good luck charm, intended to ensure the king's success in future hunts. The "Bahram Gor" silk shows the king on a lion hunt. The episode is recounted in numerous Arab chronicles: "When Bahram approached the onager, he saw that a lion had leapt onto its back, seized it between his jaws, and was preparing to break its neck. From his bow the king loosed a single arrow that plunged through both the lion's back and the onager's flank, and on into the earth. Mundsir, the king's Arab tutor, then commissioned a work showing

Byzantine silk on a Sassanid theme.

The shroud of Coire.

Byzantine silk, the shroud of Saint Victor. Eighth or ninth century. Trésor de la Cathédrale de Sens.

Buwayhid silk. Tenth or eleventh century.

Bahram mounted on horseback, killing both lion and onager with a single arrow." An attempt has obviously been made to depict the scene realistically. The galloping horse is not winged. The date palm (symbolizing the Tree of Life) bears clearly visible fruit. The large size of the medallion (33 x 35 inches) suggests that this celebration of the king's prowess may have been intended as a wall hanging. No less than ten "Bahram Gor" hunting-scene fabrics have been recorded, implying the existence of set models copied by successive weavers and goldsmiths. The same scene recurs in a Persian illumination from Firdausi's *Book of Kings*, which also alludes to Bahram Gor's fame as a great hunter.

Another piece illustrating a royal hunting scene, the Byzantine "Mozac" samite, has a border of stylized lotus flowers encircling the roundel. At the center of the repeating pattern's vertical axis is a Tree of Life. The regally mounted figure of the emperor aims a spear between a lion's gaping jaws. The immobilized horse presents all the attributes of royalty: fluttering ribbons tied to its tail, necklace around its neck, pendants hanging from its harness. The emperor is attired in a formal caftan made from a fabric richly decorated with motifs seen also on Coptic tunics.

A fine example of the same theme can be found in the eighth-century silk fragment known as the "Four Celestial Gardens" or "Shōmu Banner," a hunting-scene tapestry made by Tang dynasty weavers, and presented by Emperor Shōmu (A.D. 701–56) to the Horyuji temple in Nara (Japan). Four riders mounted on winged horses swivel in their saddles in order to aim their arrows at a springing lion. As in the Sassanid hunting scenes, the subject is shown in a beaded roundel with a Tree of Life in the center. Despite the Sassanid spirit of the piece, it can definitely be identified as Chinese because of the brand on the horse's haunch: here, a seal with Chinese characters has replaced the royal Sassanid star. The same scene was imitated with only slight variations by Japanese weavers in Nara.

A Theme Common to Both Sassanid and Byzantine Weavers

The hunting scenes and symbolic Tree of Life were often copied by Byzantine artists, and a heritage drawing on ancient Greco-Roman and Indo-European socio-religious structures was also common to both empires. This often makes accurate attribution difficult for scenes depicting a man—or men—pitted against a lion. The subject could be the Sassanid Mithras, the Greek Hercules, or a biblical hero such as Samson, David, or Daniel. In the Middle East, the legendary Mesopotamian hunter-king Gilgamesh also remained a popular subject for centuries, and was assimilated in various forms with other heroes. A silk fragment in the Vatican's Museo Sacro bears a Byzantine variation on the Sassanid theme. Two scenes are superimposed inside a roundel. The upper portion contains a central Tree of Life and a hunter wearing a short tunic and a diadem. On the diadem is the cross associated with Byzantine emperors. The hunter spears a lion who stands on its hind legs with its head turned towards him. In the lower portion, a second hunter, facing in the opposite direction, has just speared a young lion (or leopard). There is an eagle behind the animal's head and a dog between its legs. The same scene is reproduced symmetrically on the other side, producing a mirror effect.

The Byzantine tapestry known as the shroud of Coire, also called "Samson and the Lion," depicts a man dressed in a short tunic pitted against a wild animal, a scene familiar to spectators at Roman amphitheaters. Although the man could be a professional animal fighter, he might also be Samson, Hercules battling the Nemean lion, David protecting his flock from a predator, or even Daniel in the lions' den. In traditional iconography, Hercules wields a club and David a stick, so here it is reasonable to suppose that the subject is Samson, since he is wrestling with the lion as described in the Bible. The use of this silk as a shroud would tend to confirm the Samson hypothesis. Only biblical themes were considered appropriate for fabrics used in religious rites, since the fabrics themselves became sacred relics.

The shroud of Saint Victor (eighth or ninth century), today in the treasury of Sens Cathedral (France), is decorated in four elliptical roundels, measuring approximately sixteen inches in diameter, which frame a man with long hair fending off two pouncing lions. The Sassanid influence is evident in the beaded roundels and the symmetrical composition, although the theme has been freely adapted. Is this the Mesopotamian hero Gilgamesh, or Daniel in the lions' den as frequently seen in illuminated Bibles? Since the lions do not look very aggressive, and tame lions symbolize paradise regained, the hypothesis that this is a Christian hero seems plausible, though one should bear in mind that the Persian weavers who produced the cloth, probably for export, were more familiar with the legend of Gilgamesh than with the Bible. This hypothesis also applies to a fabric from the Buwayhid period (tenth to eleventh century). Muslim craftsmen often imitated Sassanid and Byzantine themes.

The "Mask" Tapestries

Numerous figured silks dating from the fifth to the seventh centuries are based on stylized female heads shown with curled hair or wearing helmets. Are these authentic Sassanid fabrics, or imitations produced in Syrian workshops? The fragments discovered during archaeological explorations in Egypt continue to pose the same problems of attribution. A Coptic fabric in shimmering colors known as the "mask" tapestry (sixth century) highlights the freedom of expression allowed by the figured-silk technique, compared with the rigidity of samites woven on draw-looms. For example, the eyes on the mask tapestries are realistic and expressive, while those on Sassanid fabrics are sometimes no more than a single dot.

The Fabulous Persian Bestiary: The Simurgh

Sassanid hunting scenes often contain winged horses with the heads of griffins or sea monsters, and other hybrid animals. But the most fabulous animal in the Persian bestiary is the simurgh, a hybrid winged dragon with the head of a dog or wolf, the talons of a falcon or vulture, and a stylized tail similar to a peacock's. The story of the simurgh—still highly popular in Iran today—is told by Firdausi in his *Book of Kings*: a boy named Zal was abandoned by his father Sam, left for dead on a mountainside, and rescued by the simurgh bird, which raised him with her own young. Here again, numerous

Byzantine fabrics illustrate different versions of the legend. Their dark colors (purple, dark green, ocher) contrast with the much lighter and subtler shades of Sassanid silks. The shroud of Saint Siviard, in the Sens Cathedral treasury, is an unusual piece. Some characteristic features of the Persian simurgh (the rosette with eight-pointed stars on the animal's haunch, the ringed tail, the shape of the wings, the beaded roundels) suggest a Sassanid provenance, but the motif inside the two beaded roundels and the special technique employed for producing this fabric indicate a Byzantine influence. A similar motif can be found on the Charlemagne shroud known as the "elephant" silk, the Byzantine provenance of which is beyond question. Furthermore, although the fabric is a damask (tone-on-tone figured raw silk), which makes the pattern difficult to decipher, each roundel contains a visible winged griffin very similar to the simurgh and—a telling detail—the bird's head, talons, and tail, as well as the starred rosette on its haunch, are embroidered in a mixture of purple silk and gold thread. These few embroidered details stand out against the solid tone-on-tone background, suggesting a stunningly effective but unfinished design.

BYZANTIUM
The Multiple Influences on Byzantine Silk

The crucible in which cultural currents from the Far East, Greece, and Rome fused was, of course, Byzantium. A typical example of Greek influence can be seen in the silk depicting Amazons, now in the Musée de Cluny, Paris. This design is similar to the Sassanid hunting scenes, but here the subjects are not male heroes, but the female warriors of classical legend. The roundel is a symmetrical, Sassanid-style composition containing two Amazons pointing their arrows at two leopards. The women are clothed in short tunics cut to reveal a single breast, reflecting the belief—as recounted by Herodotus—that Amazons routinely amputated one of their breasts in order to be able to deliver the backwards "Parthian" shot. The heads of the two figures are encircled by the ends of flowing scarfs reminiscent of the fluttering ribbons shown in depictions of Sassanid kings. The roundel is bordered by a white floral motif on a purple ground. This samite is believed to have been produced in a seventh-century Syrian workshop,

which would explain the marked Sassanid influence.

By contrast, the shroud of Saint Germain in the church of Saint Eusebius (Auxerre, France) shows the influence of imperial Rome. The pattern features a series of yellow eagles against a purple ground, and has been attributed to the imperial workshops at Constantinople.

One of the finest examples of Roman influence is an eighth-century piece known as the "quadriga" silk (Musée de Cluny), on which a charioteer is shown full-face against an imperial purple background, reining in four galloping horses. Two unmounted servants present the charioteer with a whip and a crown. Due to the optical effect of the composition, two other figures, each carrying a horn of plenty from which golden coins pour onto an altar, appear to precede the chariot. This silk, from Charlemagne's reliquary at Aachen, embodies in a single pattern all the great myths found along the Silk Road: Platonic myth (in which the horses represent the divine soul, firmly controlled and guided by the charioteer); Persian myth (Mithra rising up to heaven in the chariot of the Sun, pulled by four horses); and Buddhist myth (in which the horses represent the senses, which must be controlled by the charioteer, who represents the spirit, to prevent the chariot from being pulled off-course).

Several fragments of Byzantine narrative fabrics containing religious scenes have survived into our own time. One of these silks, illustrating the life of Saint Joseph (Sens Cathedral treasury), irresistibly recalls a modern comic strip: the three scenes are shown on horizontal bands, each with its own caption. By deciphering the inscription, scholars have been able to date this piece to sometime between the seventh and ninth centuries.

The Golden Age of Justinian the Great

Compared with the remains of clothing uncovered in Egyptian tombs, illustrations of Byzantine costume found on frescoes, illuminated manuscripts and mosaics often seem curiously stylized and conventional (unlike those depicted in Renaissance paintings, for example). It can nonetheless be useful to compare the real fabrics with their illustrations on mosaics and illuminations for documentary and dating purposes, and to gain a sense of how fashion developed in the Byzantine world.

Two celebrated mosaics (circa 548) showing Emperor Justinian (A.D. 483–565) and Empress Theodora making an offering at the church of San Vitale in Ravenna, are unusual for their detailed rendition of the figured-silk garments worn by members of the imperial court. The elaborate ornamentation of cloaks, tunics, and chlamyses produce a magnificently modulated chromatic effect in the same shades of purple, gold, amber, emerald, and sapphire found on the faded fabrics excavated from ancient tombs. The southern mosaic shows Theodora heading a procession of seven ladies-in-waiting. The narrative embroidery on her chlamys depicts the Adoration of the Magi, and is reminiscent in spirit of the "Annunciation" silk in the Vatican museum. The patterns on the robes worn by the ladies-in-waiting are varied: rosettes, scattered birds and waterfowl, and so on. The cloak worn by the woman standing next to the empress appears to be a virtually monochrome samite in pale gray on white. The visibility of its pattern increases or diminishes depending on the viewer's angle of vision, which explains the name "squint" silk coined by Arab weavers for this type of cloth. The mosaic also shows a silk drapery suspended between the small columns of the cloister.

Wresting the Secret of Sericulture from the Chinese

The Sassanids kept a firm grip on their monopoly over the silk trade with China and, as demand for the precious commodity increased, Byzantine merchants were forced to pay higher and higher prices. Meanwhile, in an attempt to expand his empire's industries, the Emperor Justinian desperately sought some way to produce this costly raw material locally. Available information on the cultivation and manufacture of silk was vague and incomplete. Greek writers believed that Chinese silk grew on "wool trees," somewhat like cotton bolls or kapok. Finally, a group of Nestorian monks from a monastery in Central Asia told the emperor the legend of a Chinese princess who a century earlier had managed to smuggle the secret of silk out of China. According to this story, the king of Khotan, also eager to obtain the secret of silk, requested the hand of a royal Chinese princess in marriage, counting on the fact that a Chinese bride would go to great lengths in order to maintain a supply of silk for her own gowns. All depended on whether his own bride would be clever enough to succeed. The king's assumption proved correct and his hopes were gratified when his bride, despite the risk involved, successfully smuggled mulberry seeds and unhatched cocoons past the Chinese border guards by hiding them in her elaborate headdress . . . which is how, according to the legend, the king of Khotan was finally able to produce silk in his own country.

The monks offered to travel to the distant land in Central Asia over which the king of Khotan had once ruled, and where silkworms had now been bred for over a century. They promised to learn the secrets of this mysterious art and bring them back to Justinian. The emperor was enthusiastic about the plan, and in turn promised to shower favors on the monks if they succeeded in their quest. According to the imperial Byzantine historian Procopius, who tells the story, the monks returned two years later, "bringing with them a large quantity of silk seeds concealed in their bamboo canes. The monks tended the seeds carefully until they hatched, and then fed the larvae day and night on a diet of mulberry leaves. Thus did sericulture come to Byzantium."

It was during the reign of Justinian I's successor, Justinian II (565–578) that silkworm breeding and the cultivation of mulberry trees spread into Syria, Calabria, Sicily, throughout the Peloponnesus, and as far as Armenia. In the words of a Persian proverb, "With time and patience the mulberry leaf turns into satin." The legend of the Chinese princess as told to Justinian by the Nestorian monks is illustrated on a wood painting, discovered near Khotan by archaeologist Sir Marc Aurel Stein, part of which is now in the British Museum. The painting shows the princess with a halo around her head. She holds a basket filled with silkworm cocoons, while a servant points to the headdress in which they were hidden.

Also of interest in this connection is a superb silk-scroll gouache in Istanbul's Topkapi palace museum, attributed to the Tabriz school and dated *circa* 1450. The nocturnal scene—servants light the way with torches and lanterns—is probably a wedding procession, very possibly to mark the marriage of a Chinese princess with one of the "barbarian" rulers of Central Asia— just as in the Nestorian monks' legend.

Coptic "mask" tapestry. Sixth century.

Fragment of a Sassanid silk discovered at Antinoopolis.

Sassanid silk with simurgh in a beaded roundel.

Byzantine "Amazon" silk. Seventh century. Musée de Cluny, Paris.

Byzantine "quadriga" silk. Eighth century. Discovered in Charlemagne's tomb. Musée de Cluny, Paris.

The shroud of Saint Germain. Seventh to eighth century. On an imperial theme. Church of Saint Eusebius, Auxerre (France).

Byzantine silk with scene of the Annunciation; an example of early Christian influence. Seventh century.

Panel showing the Chinese princess who smuggled silkworms into Khotan. British Museum, London.

Persian miniature from
Firdausi's *Book of Kings*.

Byzantine silk, known as
the "Charlemagne" shroud.

Byzantine "elephant" silk.
Abegg-Stiftung, Switzeland.

Fragment of a multicolored samite, the shroud of Saint
Josse, from Khorasan. Persia, mid-tenth century.

Fragment known as the
"Kayqubd" silk. Anatolian,
thirteenth century.

Fresco in the Dunhuang caves showing Silk Road merchants from across
the known world. Seventh to ninth century.

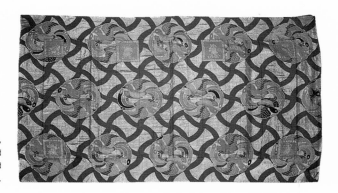

Seven-band *kesa*,
silk and laminated
gilt paper with bird
motif. Sixth century.

ISLAM AND BYZANTIUM

Following a century of victorious Islamic
conquests, the newly rich Muslim caliphs
and traders sought to recreate, in their
mansions and palaces, the interiors of the
desert tents they had lived in as nomads.
Decorative effects in harmonious repeat
patterns were used abundantly on the flat
surfaces of enamels, ceramics, and, above
all, textiles. The magnificence of this
decorative art led Arabian studies specialist
Maurice Lombard to call Islam a "textile
civilization." The patronage of Muslim
princes spurred silk and wool weavers to
develop new decorative themes, and the
yearning of the former nomads for the cool
repose of verdant gardens after a life spent
on the desert sands is reflected in the
designs on numerous fabrics and carpets.
Meanwhile, despite the growing influence
of Islam throughout the empire, Byzantine
art continued to develop, although official
imperial art fell under the sway of the
intensified middle-eastern influence now
coming from Islamic Persia (for example,
the purple-ground "quadriga" silk
described above).

The Elephant Road

The "elephant" shroud that was used to
wrap Charlemagne's relics could only have
been woven in the imperial workshops of
Constantinople, which specialized in the
manufacture of fabrics with a royal purple
ground, which were presented as gifts
from the Byzantine emperor to foreign
sovereigns, popes, and bishops. The
shroud's provenance is further confirmed
by the Greek inscription on its lower
border. It was in the year 1000 that Holy
Roman Emperor Otto III had
Charlemagne's tomb opened so that the
precious relics within could be wrapped in
the shroud, probably chosen to
commemorate the elephant presented to
Charlemagne by the great caliph Harun al-
Rashid (764?–809). In the East, elephants
were the preferred mount of kings and
symbolized regal power. The Sassanids, in
their wars against the Byzantines, first
pioneered the use of combat elephants
sheathed in metal armor, caparisoned with
leopard skins and cloth of silk and gold,
and carrying howdahs filled with archers.

A Byzantine "elephant" silk at the Abegg-Stiftung in Switzerland, shows these animals caparisoned with gold and silk in the Sassanid style, but the geometric composition of the roundel is already Islamic in spirit.

The Islamic influence is even more apparent on the shroud of Saint Josse (from the church of the same name, in the Pas-de-Calais region of northern France, and now in the Louvre) which dates from 961 A.D. This shroud was woven in Khorasan and bears an inscription in Kufic characters: "Glory and prosperity to Qu'id Abu Mansur Bakh-takin, may Allah prolong his existence."

The elephant motif recurs on another Byzantine silk evoking the origins of the Silk Road and its close links, through Buddhism, with the Elephant Road. Although the elephant is primarily a symbol of indomitable strength, in legend it is also associated with the birth of the Buddha, whose mother Queen Maya is said to have been impregnated by a young elephant. Buddhism was a major influence along the road, which also served as a vector for the dissemination of the great religions.

THE FAR EAST
Tang and Song Dynasty China

The Byzantine Empire owed its unity in large part to a common language, Arabic, and a common faith, Islam. Tang dynasty China was cemented by its expanding silk and porcelain trade, and by the spread of Buddhism, the common religion of the peoples of Central Asia. As a major trading route, the Silk Road played a decisive role in propagating the art and philosophy of Buddhism, a pacifist doctrine that originated in northeast India during the sixth century B.C. The spread of Buddhism generated a heavy traffic of pilgrims and missionaries traveling between India, China, and Central Asia, with the city of Dunhuang as the region's major cultural and religious center.

A late Tang dynasty mural discovered in a cave near Dunhuang shows the armies of Zhang Yiuchao regrouping in order to reconquer lost territories and re-establish the free movement of goods and people over the Silk Road. Elsewhere, a fresco depicts the traders, travelers, pilgrims, and emissaries who used the Road: Turks, Arabs, Persians, and black Africans.

In another painting, we see the Buddhist monk Xuan Zang on his triumphal return from his voyage to the Indies being greeted by lines of court officials and priests. Pack horses carry the Sutras, or sacred Indian texts, he has brought back for the emperor.

Among other developments representative of the new, extremely varied textiles woven under the Chinese Tang and Song dynasties were the distinctive *kesi* silks. All-silk tapestries had already been woven by Han artisans, but during the Tang dynasty the weave was considerably refined. Up to sixty-six threads were used per inch for the warp and up to three hundred eighty for the weft, a split-tapestry technique representing amazing skill and progress.

Tapestries from this period were used as bindings for religious books and scrolls, as decoration in palaces, and occasionally for making imperial robes. The weave was fine enough to reproduce works of art, and some artists even took up the study of tapestry in order to execute their own works directly in cloth.

The Maritime Silk Route between China and Japan

The Chinese draw-loom was introduced into Japan during the fifth century by Korean immigrants (or prisoners-of-war) who had learned the technique during the Chinese conquest of their own country. Although sericulture spread quickly, Japan did not fully become open to Chinese cultural influences until the reign of the Tang dynasty in China, and the Nara period (A.D. 646–794) in Japan.

The treasure of Emperor Shōmu is preserved in the Shōsō-in repository at the Tōdai-ji Temple, one of the oldest in Japan. The repository contains thousands of precious objects, many of which were carried over the Silk Road from Syria, Greece, Persia, India, and other lands. Most important is the textile collection, which includes magnificent silks from China and other Asian countries. During the fifteenth century, Japanese silk weavers settled in the Nishijin section of Kyoto, where weaving workshops can still be found today.

The Kesa, Symbol of the Silk Road

When Buddhist monks from India and China reached Japan in the sixth century, they brought with them their ritual costume, the *kesa*, a kind of patchwork mantle or shawl that was passed down from master to disciple. Families seeking to ensure repose for the souls of their loved ones presented pieces of cloth (silks, tapestries, and embroideries) to the Buddhist temples to be transformed into *kesas* or banners.

The early Buddhists had strict rules governing use of these pieces of fabric by the monks, whose duty it was to "wash them, dye them, and sew them, so that they formed a garment with a perfectly defined composition." As a group, these time-worn silk patchworks, executed in a range of styles and techniques, constitute an eloquent symbol of the Silk Route and Buddhism. Today only fragments of the patterns woven into these figured silks have survived. A few faded peony petals, part of a mythical dragon or phoenix, or the merest outline of a cloud add to the magical aura of these symbolic creations. During the fourteenth century, sumptuous silks designed by Japanese weavers were used to make kimonos, costumes for Nō drama, and Samurai uniforms. The Japanese textile tradition continued to flourish in the eighteenth and nineteenth centuries, and in the twentieth century Japanese design has had a major influence on art and interior decoration in the West.

ISLAM AND THE WEST
The Silk Road Extends Westward

Capital of the Abbassid Empire (A.D. 750–1258), Baghdad became a center for all the major trade routes of Asia, Europe, and Africa. The golden age of the Abbassid dynasty was during the reign of Harun al-Rashid, whose opulent court was later described in *The Thousand and One Nights*. The fame of Harun al-Rashid's kingdom traveled far beyond its frontiers, and ambassadors visited his court from places as far-off as Tang dynasty China and Charlemagne's Holy Roman Empire. The silks produced in the caliph's workshops (known as *tiraz*) illustrate the syncretism of Indo-Persian and Hellenist influences grafted onto Islamic and Arabian culture.

The "lion" shroud in the Sens Cathedral treasury is an outstanding example of Islamic influence. The Sassanid motif of confronted lions separated by a central axis appears in pearled roundels. This silk, once severed in two, can now be seen in its entirety: the upper portion was discovered in the reliquary of Saint Colomba, and the lower in 1896, in a coffin holding the body of Saint Loup.

Under the rule of the Fatimid dynasty (A.D. 909–1171), Cairo rivaled Cordoba and Baghdad in the sumptuous decoration of its mosques and palaces, but only fragments of the Fatimid weavers' work has survived. These include remnants of fabrics woven in *tiraz* factories for ceremonial and ritual garments and a few tapestries, some in traditional wool but many in multicolored silk. Ancient geometric Coptic motifs were ideally adapted to the Islamic preference for abstract images.

Cordoba, ruled by the Umayyad caliphate from A.D. 756, became an international artistic and intellectual center famed for its poets, philosophers, and musicians. The caliph, Abd al-Rahman, encouraged the expansion of sericulture throughout Moorish Spain. This local silk provided a direct supply for the *tiraz* factories set up by Syrian weavers who had brought their Chinese-style draw-looms to Spain and North Africa. It had thus taken this sophisticated technology some twelve centuries to travel from China to Europe— and even when it finally did arrive, it was confined to the Muslim world.

Only a few of the silks woven under the Buwayhid and Samanid dynasties of Islamic Persia have survived; all we have today are fragments such as the "elephant" silk and the shroud of Saint Josse. However, in 1925 a trove of Buwayhid silks was discovered in tombs adjacent to the sanctuary of Shahr-Bānū, near the ancient city of Rayy, just a few miles from Teheran. Most of the motifs are based on animal subjects, and there is a clear Sassanid influence. Here we again meet the simurgh; and also the legendary green bird reputed to shelter denizens of the other world in its crop (also depicted on the ceiling mosaics of the Palatine chapel in Palermo, Sicily.)

"Lion" shroud, showing Muslim influence. Trésor de la Cathédrale de Sens.

Coptic tapestry with dancers.

THE CRUSADES

The crusades heralded an entirely new phase in the relationship between Christian West and Islamic East. When the European crusaders arrived in the Middle East, they were stunned by the wealth of this new-found civilization and immediately attempted to colonize it on the pretext of recovering the Holy Land from the Muslims. The crusaders attacked mercilessly wherever they encountered opposition, whether Muslim or Byzantine. The sack of Constantinople in 1204 was a particularly grievous example. Despite the destruction wrought, the crusades brought Europeans in contact with eastern cultures, giving a fresh impetus to western decorative arts.

The patterns and motifs found on oriental fabrics, and on Islamic and Byzantine art works as a whole, had an especially strong influence on the European artisans who carved the capitals of columns used in Romanesque cathedrals. Over a span of three centuries (1050–1350), thousands of cathedrals, churches, monasteries, and abbeys were constructed in Christian Europe. The artisans who built them belonged to religious brotherhoods with which they traveled from one construction site to another, not only throughout Europe, but also in Syria, Palestine, and Egypt. These European craftsmen were allowed to move freely through the Muslim world, where they discovered the superb architecture of the great mosques in Cairo, Kairouan, Fez, and Cordoba.

The walls of mosques and European cathedrals are decorated with the same geometric designs—chevrons, rosettes, florets, palmettes, and so on—that had been characteristic of textile design from its beginnings. Craftsmen, whether sculptors, glass blowers, enamelers, weavers, or illuminators, all drew on the same themes (Good versus Evil) and from the same fabulous bestiaries that had first appeared in Chinese and Sassanid textile art. The ancient dragons, simurghs, and monsters reappeared in terrifying visions of the Apocalypse, and classic scenes of struggle between legendary or biblical heroes and hybrid animals were rendered even more fantastic by the use of bright oriental colors.

The Mongol Occupation

When, in 1211, Genghis Khan launched the Mongolian campaign to conquer both Europe and Asia, and to create an empire stretching from Peking to the Atlantic Ocean, the Silk Road became a path of blood and fear. However, on his death in 1227, the great leader bequeathed to his four sons the most extensive empire the world had ever known. Although he had not succeeded in conquering western Europe, he had as good as fulfilled Alexander the Great's dream of uniting Asia with the West. When Baghdad fell, the frontiers that had once divided the Silk Road from the China Sea to the Black Sea disappeared. This stunning turn of events finally opened first Asia, and then the Far East to the Europeans. Emissaries from the pope and the French king, such as Franciscan monks Jean Plan du Carpin and Guillaume de Rubroek, were the first western Europeans to venture onto this *terra incognita*, accurate descriptions of which they brought home with them. Meanwhile, the crusades had contributed to the expansion of Italian trading centers such as Genoa, Pisa, and above all Venice, which in the thirteenth century was at the apex of its power. The *pax mongolica* made it possible for ambassadors, merchants, and missionaries to travel safely all the way from Baghdad to Peking.

The Polo Brothers Discover Mongol China

Thanks to the written account left by Marco Polo, we are familiar with the fabulous adventure undertaken by his father and uncle, the first Venetian (or European) merchants ever to explore China. He himself accompanied them on their second expedition, which lasted sixteen years. The journey was later described by Marco Polo in his *Book of Travels,* a work teeming with wonderful stories, some of them repeated in *The Thousand and One Nights.*

Marco Polo's descriptions—whether accurate or embroidered—attracted many thirteenth- and fourteenth-century merchants to China, in search not of silk, but of gold and precious gems. These feverish explorers were joined in the late fifteenth century by the great Portuguese navigators.

Miniature from *L'Histoire du Saint-Graal.* Thirteenth century.

Hispano-Mauresque lampas silk. Fifteenth century. Lozenges and bars on twill background.

Engraving of a caravan.

Fabulous beasts from a fourteenth-century edition of Marco Polo's *Book of Travels.*

Watercolor showing Marco Polo dressed as a Tartar. Eighteenth century.

Miniature by the official painter to Charles of Angoulême. *c.* 1480. From *Secrets de l'histoire naturelle.*

23

Mosaic in the Roger II room at the Norman palace, Palermo.

Palermo altar cloth. Sicily, twelfth century. Yellow silk with a motif of confronted birds and leopards embroidered in gold.

Palermo influenced silk, known as the "Potentien" shroud.

Shroud with peacocks, known as "King Robert's Cope." Spanish, twelfth century.

Wilton Diptych. c. 1395. National Gallery, London.

Fatimid influenced silk. Eleventh century.

Antonio del Pollaiuolo, *Portrait of Galeazzo Maria Sforza*. 1471. Galleria degli Uffizi, Florence.

Palermo, Gateway to East and West

Palermo played a crucial role in the spread of sericulture and fine figured-silk weaving into Italy and France. In 1072, contacts between East and West were widened through the invasion of Sicily by the Normans, who supported and developed the manufacture of Palermo silks, developing the craft both technically and artistically.

The mosaics in the Palatine chapel and the private royal chapel of Roger II in the Norman palace of Palermo contain numerous imitations of Sassanid and Byzantine motifs, an indication of the religious and cultural eclecticism common during this period of Sicilian history. These mosaics are probably the work of Saracen artisans trained by the Byzantines, thus forming a distinctive Sicilian school in Palermo and Monreale. A typical example of the style can be seen in the Arabo-Norman architecture of the palace built by Roger II.

One of these mosaics has a roundel motif on a gilt background containing lions, griffins and hunting scenes in exotic gardens; animals facing one another separated by a Tree of Life; and a man, who could be either Gilgamesh or Samson, clutching two lions by the neck.

Motifs and patterns from Islamic silks were a rich source of inspiration for medieval mosaic makers. The Muslims who remained in Palermo were treated with the same tolerance shown to Christians in Moorish Spain, and there is a strong similarity between Hispano-Mauresque and Arabo-Norman art. Historian and cartographer al-Idrisi embodies this melding of the Christian and Muslim worlds in Palermo. After studying in Cordoba, he settled in Palermo, where Roger II commissioned him to construct a huge annotated planisphere. "On it," writes al-Idrisi, "were the regions with their countries and cities, the rivers, lands, and seas, the distances between them, the roads, and all the local sights."

The influence of pre-Norman civilizations in Sicily is evident on the silk shroud found in the "Potentien" reliquary (Sens Cathedral treasury). The basic motif is a Chinese-style roundel containing two confronted eagles and two griffins separated by a highly stylized Tree of Life. The talons and beaks of the mythical birds and beasts are accented in red to contrast with the deep blue and turquoise of the pattern as a whole. The borders of the roundels contain the earliest known inscriptions in *nakshi* script, a decorative calligraphy found on numerous fourteenth-century Italian silks.

The oriental influence on Palermo silks can also be seen in the Wilton diptych, painted in France *circa* 1395. This work illustrates the coronation of Richard II of England. In the background stand Saint John the Baptist, Edward the Confessor and Saint Edward. Saint Edward's ankle-length cope is draped with a blue and gold silk embroidered in a bird motif. Richard II, kneeling in the foreground, wears a red and gold silk cope with roundels containing a stag.

The similarity between the "Potentien" shroud and the "Peacock" cope of Robert of Anjou in the basilica of Saint-Sernin (Toulouse, France) underscores the relationship between the patterns used for textiles and those used for decorative mosaics in the palaces of the Norman kings. Although this samite is frequently attributed a thirteenth-century Spanish origin, the confronted peacocks separated by a Tree of Life bear a definite similarity to the motifs found on mosaics in the Palatine chapel. On the top and bottom of the pearled roundel an inscription in *nakshi* script confirms the Muslim influence, which was as strong in Sicily as in Moorish Spain. Although the Fatimid influence is especially marked on the cope of Saint Mexme (Chinon, France; eleventh century), which shows a bird attacking two confronted chained leopards with cubs flanking a small Tree of Life, the Sicilian provenance of the piece is borne out by its similarity to a mosaic in the bedchamber of Roger II, on which two confronted lions with turned heads are shown in the same position, executed in the same style.

Frederick II and Charles of Anjou

The reign of Frederick II of Hohenstaufen (1194–1250) over Sicily ushered in a period of intense artistic ferment. A cultivated man keenly interested in Islamic mysticism, Frederick supported Palermo as an artistic center, bringing together eastern and western cultures.

In 1266, Charles of Anjou, brother of the French king Louis IX, was crowned king of Sicily by the pope. Just as Charles was preparing to invade the Byzantine empire, eight thousand French inhabitants of Sicily were massacred during the April 28 (Easter Monday) uprising. The exodus that followed sent Muslim silk weavers to

Almeria, Spain; and non-Muslim weavers—primarily Jewish—to Lucca in Italy. The uprising was a protest against the brutal treatment meted out to local Sicilians by Charles of Anjou's troops.

The decline of Sicily and exodus of the city's skilled craftsmen led to Lucca's role as the new capital of the European silk industry, which then began to spread gradually to all of western Christendom. The few silks that have survived from this period illustrate the degree to which Sicily, a focal point in the Mediterranean Sea linked directly to both Italian and Arab ports, united all the traditions represented by the Silk Road—Sassanid, Byzantine, Coptic, Berber, Muslim, and Chinese. This was the crucible in which Italian textile art was formed. The familiar fleur-de-lis motif, eventually chosen by the French royal family for its coat of arms, was originally designed by Palermo weavers during the French occupation of Sicily. In the early Palermo versions, the fleur-de-lis appears in either a scatter pattern, or framed in losange-shaped escutcheons. However, the heraldic fleur-de-lis motif was commonly used in fifteenth-century Italy for ordinary decoration. For example, in Pollaiuolo's portrait of Galeazzo Sforza, the duke of Milan is shown wearing an emerald-green doublet embroidered with a golden fleur-de-lis design—although this may be a subtle allusion to the Sforza family's hatred of their French rival, Louis XII.

Discovery of a Direct Sea Route to Europe from China and the East Indies

As western Europeans gradually learned about the wonders of the East—in part through the glowing descriptions of pioneering travelers like Marco Polo—European navigators became more daring, venturing outside familiar local sea routes in an attempt to find a direct maritime passage to the fabulous treasures of Cathay and the Indies. Although since the time of Ptolemy geographers had believed the Indian Ocean to be land-locked, the fifteenth-century European explorers set out to prove the opposite.

Christopher Columbus, the son of a Genoese weaver, is said to have read the condensed 1485 Antwerp edition of Marco Polo's *Description of the World*, underlining passages referring to gold, precious gems, pearls, and spices. Columbus believed in the existence of a direct western sea route to the wealth of the Indies, and in his log of

the journey, he compared his own discoveries with Marco Polo's reports, on the assumption that he was traveling over some of the same ground. His assumption was mistaken, but his little fleet did eventually open up a path to wealth—the wealth of the Americas.

Vasco da Gama's Amazing Discovery

On 4 May 1493, yielding to pressure from Spain, Pope Alexander VI decreed the division of the world in two. All lands located to the west of the meridian—i.e. west of the Azores—would belong to Spain; those to the east, including Africa and Asia, would belong to Portugal. The two parties to the agreement subsequently decided to shift the meridian slightly to the west, which six months later resulted in Portugal's acquisition of Brazil.

In 1498, the route to the Indies was discovered by the Portuguese navigator Vasco da Gama. This discovery, added to that of Brazil, extended the power of tiny Portugal to the frontiers of the known world, a situation that was to last for almost a century.

At the time of Vasco da Gama's arrival in the East, Arab traders still controlled an import-export monopoly with India. Pepper and other spices were carried overland to Jiddah, sent across the Red Sea, and then taken by caravan to Mediterranean ports, where Venetian ships picked them up and carried them to southern Europe. Portugal's goal, in order to lower prices and thus gain control of this vast market, was to break up the monopoly controlled by the Muslim merchants.

When Vasco da Gama returned to Portugal after a voyage lasting two years, he brought with him goods from Calicut on the eastern coast of India, purchased on behalf of the king of Portugal, Manuel I: pepper, musk and other spices, pearls and precious gems, and silks and porcelains. The sea route to the Indies had been discovered.

Early Portuguese navigators jealously guarded the "secret" of their new sea route, which remained a mystery to many inlanders. An object illustrating this bafflement is a late sixteenth-century Persian carpet showing Portuguese ships with a strange-looking crew aboard. The Persian weavers used their imaginations to depict the newfound route and its masters, neither of which they had ever actually seen.

Silk Weaving
in Europe

—

B

Veronese, *Vision of Saint Helena*. Sixteenth century. Pinacoteca, Vatican. Veronese consistently achieved subtle contrasts between the colors of the silks and velvets worn by his subjects and the darker hues of background hangings.

y the end of the thirteenth century, the Italian city of Lucca had become an internationally renowned center for the manufacture and commerce of fine silk. Lucca's silk merchants had agents and outlets in many European cities, and they also attended all the market fairs in Champagne, where the phrase "Good silk is Lucca silk" had become axiomatic. The raw silk used by Lucca weavers was imported from Asia. The brilliant white variety from China, although actually less expensive, was considered far superior to other grades from Persia and Syria. A contemporary ledger notes: "A price of five francs two sous per pound for undyed Chinese silk compared with seven francs ten sous for silk not from Cathay."

The magnificent finished silk cloth from China sold throughout Europe at the time of the Mongol Empire was imported through Persia. Today, fragments of these silks can be seen in many church treasuries. Frederick II's policies increased contacts between Lucca and the Muslim countries of the Middle East and Spain, and this may explain the use of oriental patterns and motifs reminiscent of the Sassanid style on Lucca silks. One example is the *chi* motif used in some religious scenes to represent heavenly bliss and divine grace. Another, visible on a piece at the Musée de Cluny, Paris, is the alternating pattern of angels hovering above a ribbon of interlaced clouds on a star-studded purple background.

Lucca Silk

An oriental influence is also evident in less formal compositions, where a sense of movement is achieved through the use of asymmetrical repeat patterns, often copied from Chinese or Sassanid bestiaries. These patterns are surrounded with luminous, curling scrolls similar in effect to the sinuous veils of sacred Buddhist dancers shown on the Dunhuang frescoes. Contemporary inventories list Lucca silks containing griffins, gazelles, and eagles (often mistaken for dragons) with wings and talons embroidered in gold thread according to a Persian technique: the thread in fact consisted of a very thin strip of laminated gold wire which, to quote a contemporary account, was "wound around a heart of gold-beater's skin." In modern terms: wound onto a shuttle around a core (heart) of animal gut.

Lucca silks also show a marked Palermo influence, presumably due to the influx of weavers who were forced to leave the Sicilian capital after the revolt against the French. Definitive attribution is thus made doubly difficult, especially since Lucca figured silks became so famous that the name was soon used to describe any high-quality Italian silk.

At the height of Lucca's renown, the city contained over three thousand silk-weaving looms. The city was best known for the manufacture of figured nacre silk in tone-on-tone green, or white patterns executed in lustrous satin on tightly-woven, almost opaque taffeta. The contrast between the two weaves and their different textures produced the characteristic mother-of-pearl effect, found also on certain fourteenth-century porcelain wares. In 1314, Lucca was sacked by the pro-imperialilst forces commanded by the Pisan Ghibelline Uguccione della Faggiuola, and all the

papal supporting Guelph weavers were forced to flee. Most eventually settled in Venice and Florence. After several years of bloody political conflict, peace was finally restored to Lucca and the silk industry began to expand once more. When the French king, Charles VIII made his triumphal entry into the city, he was welcomed by a crowd of "merchant princes and other inhabitants of said city who, as a rare honor, were accoutred and dressed in fine cloths of gold and velvet."

Venice, European Capital of the Silk Road

Venice had always played a key role in the transport and commerce of luxury goods carried by caravan over the silk routes of Asia, and it now became the international capital for the gold, spice, and silk trade. Bales of raw silk were sent by caravan through Syria, stopping along the way at cities such as Aleppo, where they were heavily taxed. At the end of the overland journey, the bales were loaded onto Venetian ships at Antioch and Alexandria and sent across the Mediterranean Sea to Europe. Venice was already a thriving silk-weaving center when the artisans fleeing Lucca arrived early in the fourteenth century. The newcomers were granted loans repayable in finished fabric, and accommodation was found for them in the Santa Maria dei Servi quarter of the city. The Lucca weavers, who formed their own guild in 1349, brought new life to Venetian textile design. Because of its close ties with the Orient, the Serenissima enjoyed the privilege of trading throughout Byzantium without paying taxes. The Venetians also owned their own silk-weaving workshops in Byzantium and Syria. These interrelationships fostered an active exchange of the techniques and patterns stored in the "memory" of the Silk Road.

Cap worn by a Venetian dignitary. Twelfth century. Chiesa dei Gesuati (Santa Maria Assunta), Venice.

A typical Venetian *ferronnerie* or antique ciselé velvet. Fifteenth century. Musée des Arts de la Mode et du Textile (collection UCAD), Paris.

Right:
Genoa ciselé velvet. Sixteenth century. Georges Le Manach archives, Tours.

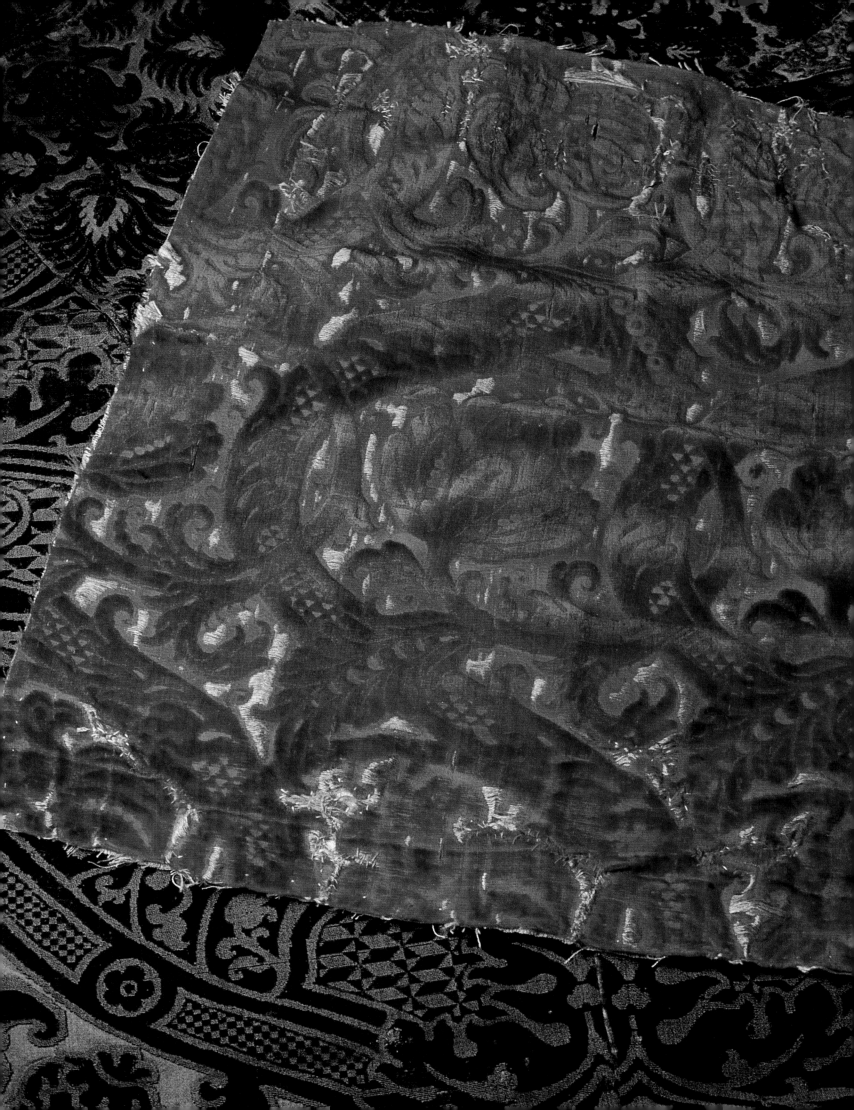

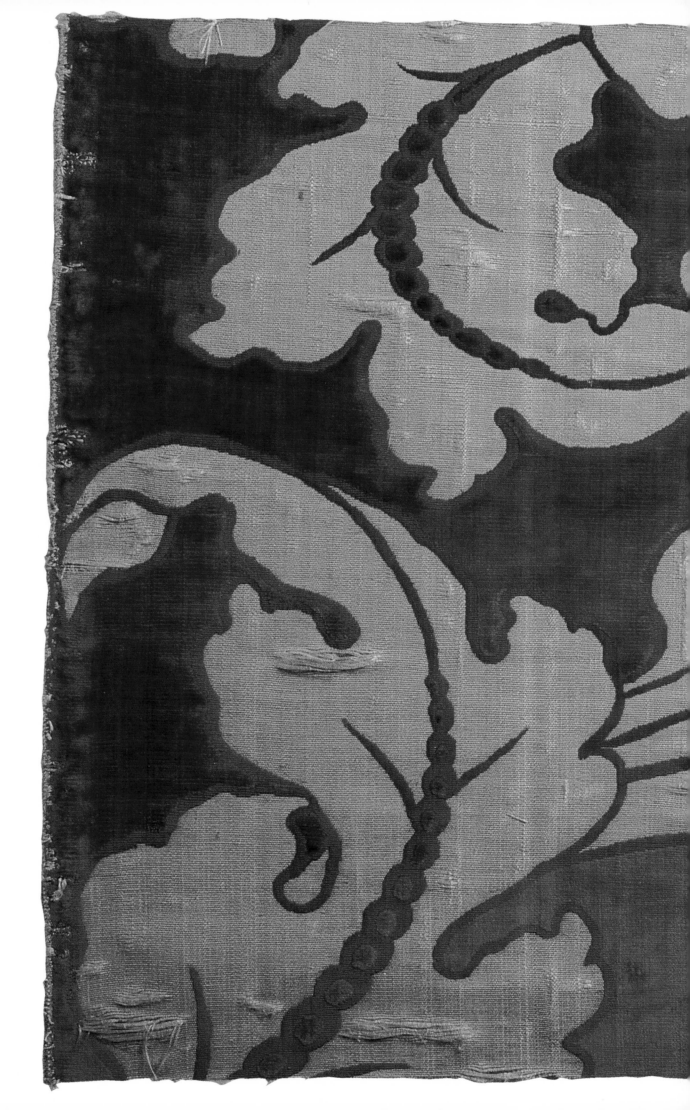

Italian ciselé velvet. Fifteenth century. Ratti archives, Como.

VENETIAN VELVET IN RENAISSANCE PAINTINGS. The technique for weaving velvet was invented in China during the Western Han period (206 B.C.–A.D. 9), a development confirmed by Ibn Battuta, who reports on the manufacture of "damasked velvet fabrics" in the city of Zayton (today Quanzhou). It is probable that the technique was introduced into Italy by Persian exiles who chose to settle in Venice because of the city's commercial contacts with Asia Minor. The word "velvet" comes from the Old French *veluotte* (twelfth century) by way of the Latin *villutus*, from *villus*, meaning "shaggy hair." The term refers to the fact that velvets are woven by picking long weft loops through the warp threads, thus creating a heavy pile.

Gold-piqué velvet was a Venetian invention clearly influenced by the magnificently luminous and colorful mosaics of Saint Mark's Basilica, and their profusion of golden tesserae. Fifteenth-century ciselé velvets provide fine examples of the way in which weavers exploited the contrast between the luminosity of gold and the dark red or green background of the velvet.

Ciselé velvet was one of the most original of all Venetian inventions. This technique involves shearing the pile loops on the fabric warp to different heights (referred to as *alto-basso*) in order to create a variety of intricately textured patterns. The contrast between the velvety surface of the pattern and the matte background of the woven fabric produces shimmering effects in silken shades of red, purple, and turquoise blue.

Most prized of all, however, were the *ferronnerie* (ironwork) or antique velvets. These were solid emerald green or ruby red velvets into which was cut a linear pattern imitating the wrought-iron or stone mullions in the windows of Gothic churches. The contrast between the light color of the underlying satin and the deep shades of the shorn velvet produced unprecedented textured effects.

One example of antique velvet with fifteenth-century floral patterns worked in gold can be seen in the Virgin's robe in Carlo Crivelli's *Virgin and Child Enthroned with Saints*. Italian Renaissance painters from Masaccio to Pisanello, depicted their influential sitters clothed in sumptuous robes of ciselé velvet.

Carlo Crivelli, *Virgin and Child.*
Fifteenth century. Pinacoteca
di Brera, Milan.

Scutari in the Balkans. These patterns were copied by Italian weavers, who incorporated them into new decorative compositions based on western European designs. One such adaptation can be seen on a polychrome velvet at Musée Historique des Tissus in Lyon. The pattern of birds perched on flowering branches is Persian in spirit, but here it is treated in the classic style of Renaissance Europe. Some Venetian velvets have an oriental dragon motif in a symmetrical reversed S-shaped composition framed by flowerets. A brocaded fifteenth-century Venetian dalmatic provides another example of the oriental influence, with a pattern of sinuous grape vines framing alternating dragons and griffins reminiscent of the long-tailed Persian simurgh.

A magnificent early fifteenth-century Venetian lampas silk resembles ciselé velvet because of the dramatic contrast between the yellow background and the dark green pattern. Within a pattern of palmettes—which could be a distant reference to the Tree of Life—we recognize the fabulous lions and eagles with their radiant aureoles found in Sassanid and Chinese bestiaries. Some of the decorative floral motifs are reworked in white or blue embroidery, creating a sharp contrast with the muted golds and greens of this Lucca-style Venetian silk.

The Venetian silk industry maintained its success for a time, but ultimately succumbed to the strong competition from other Italian cities. During the fifteenth century there were ten thousand active looms in Venice, but by the end of the sixteenth only three thousand remained. This decline was further hastened by the development of silk weaving to the north, in the French city of Lyon.

VENETIAN AND FLORENTINE VELVET IN FLEMISH PAINTINGS. Italian painters were not the only artists inspired by Venetian velvets. Renaissance Flemish painters such as Jan van Eyck and Hans Memling depicted velvets and brocades in their subjects' clothing, as well as baldachins and canopies. It is also said that, even well into the seventeenth century, Anthony van Dyck kept a collection of Venetian and Florentine fabrics in his studio to use as models in his compositions. The *Virgin with Chancellor Rolin* was commissioned from Jan van Eyck by Chancellor Nicolas Rolin of Burgundy for his private chapel in the church at Autun. In this painting, the Virgin Mary is enveloped in a voluminous red cloak trimmed with gold and pearls. Chancellor Rolin, who kneels before her, wears a magnificent fur-trimmed velvet cloak with a large gold bouclé floral motif on a purple ground. This Venetian velvet is strongly reminiscent of a sixteenth-century altar cloth in the Cini collection. The same pattern

Florentine brocade. Fifteenth century. Museo Nazionale del Bargello, Florence.
An example of the Byzantine-style use of gold to highlight patterns. This silk was restored by Lisio of Florence.

An accurate illustration of the opulence characteristic of Florentine festivals can be seen on the panels of a wedding chest showing the marriage of Broccacio Adimari, painted by an anonymous fifteenth-century master and now in the Accademia, Florence. Particularly remarkable are the dresses with trains, one a gold brocade on an almost-black background, the other a silver brocade with golden pastilles on a green background dotted with black.

THE ART OF SILK IN FLORENCE. Fourteenth-century Florence attracted merchants from every corner of the Orient. It was renowned for its artistry in silk, or "arte di por Santa Maria"—a reference to the section of the city where this powerful merchant guild had its headquarters. Illuminations from a 1487 treatise on the art of silk, now in the Laurentian Library, show each step in the manufacture of silk fabric, from spooling, to dyeing, to weaving.

If we compare this treatise with silk-weaving scenes in Chinese manuscripts, we see that the basic techniques remained virtually unchanged except for the addition of new throwing machines. In a letter addressed to the Venetian merchants, who had slighted their Florentine counterparts, one Benedetto Dei lists all the fabrics manufactured in his city: gold brocades, silks, damasks, satins. He concludes on a challenging note: "We make, have made, and will always make much more than your cities of Venice and Genoa and Lucca put together." Florence specialized in the manufacture of splendid silk-and-gold brocades and its magnificent floral and foliage patterns inspired many early Italian painters including Giotto and Botticelli. Ciselé velvet, on the other hand, was imported from Venice and Genoa. In Bronzino's portrait of Eleonora of Toledo, the fabric used for the subject's costume—a ciselé velvet decorated in moss-green floral patterns with gold and silver curlicues—is probably Genoese.

Right:
Lampas coat of arms silk. Sixteenth century. Reproduction by Lisio of Florence. This lampas silk was described by a chronicler reporting on the marriage of Francesco de Medici and Bianca Cappello in October 1579: "One platform was built higher than the others and draped in cloths of silk and gold embroidered with the coat of arms granted to Bianca by the Serenissima: the Medici globes, the lion of Saint Mark, and the Cappello helmet, surmounted by a royal crown and supported by two graceful female figures."

Brocade with small gold-embroidered floral motifs. Fifteenth century.

The links between textile art and painting are especially marked in silk-embroidered fabrics from Tuscany. Embroiderers were influenced by painters, and vice versa. Tuscan embroiderers attempted to rival the chiaroscuro of Renaissance paintings, and relied on artists' designs for inspiration. This tendency is borne out by a pen-and-ink design on linen, now at the museum of works from Orvieto Cathedral, which was executed by Ugolino di Prete Ilario for an embroiderer friend. Several embroidery techniques were sometimes combined on a single vestment.

Gold-bouclé velvet, perhaps Florentine. Sixteenth century. Museo Nazionale del Bargello, Florence. The pattern is very similar to the one on Eleonora of Toledo's gown in the Bronzino portrait.

The Orvieto dalmatic, for example, is a classic red velvet with a gold-embroidered pomegranate motif that also includes Nativity scenes. As for the influence of embroiderers on artists, although Botticelli has frequently been credited with designing the embroidery patterns in his paintings (such as the floral motifs on the dress worn by the subject of *Spring*), more often than not it was the artist who copied designs originating with the embroiderers. Another example, the parrots, hares, and tortoises with floral tendrils on the mantle in Orcagna's *Coronation of the Virgin*, dating from the mid-fourteenth century, could have been copied straight from a Coptic tapestry.

Caftan attributed to Somain II. Topkapi Saray Müzesi, Istanbul. Ciselé velvet on gold ground, silver-embroidered lobed roundels containing stylized lotus flowers.

Many other Italian cities boasted important textile industries. Sienna specialized in figured fabrics on religious themes that rivaled embroidered ecclesiastical vestments. Genoa was famed for its ciselé velvets with patterns of tulips, carnations, and hyacinths on yellow silk. Perugia was known for figured ecru linen altar cloths embroidered in turquoise-blue cotton. These stylized friezes depict all the fabulous beasts familiar from the Silk Road—lions, dragons, stags, eagles—and also knights, ladies, and falconry scenes. Last but not least, Milan attracted large numbers of velvet weavers by extending special privileges to them, but many later left for Lyon, lured by the French king François I's promises of even greater privileges.

Right:
Bronzino, *Eleonora of Toledo with her son Giovanni. c. 1545*. Galleria degli Uffizi, Florence. The meticulous design of the garment highlights the contrast between the various velvet techniques. Eleonora of Toledo was buried in this gown.

THE SILK INDUSTRY
IN TOURS AND LYON

Noble and royal patronage in France, extended first by Charles VII and then by his son Louis XI, served as the major impetus for the dramatic growth of the French silk-weaving industry during the fifteenth century. After one hundred years of internecine warfare, France, under Louis XI, began to recover from past ordeals—war, famine, plague, and uprisings by peasants and artisans. The possessions of the duchy of Burgundy within the borders of France reverted to the French crown. The king seized the opportunity offered by peace and stability to encourage the expansion of trade "both on sea and on land and in all countries, kingdoms, and dukedoms." One of his goals was to bring to France the craft of weaving fine Italian figured silks and ciselé velvets, in order to stop the "drain of gold and silver from our coffers" caused by the massive import of foreign textiles. After consulting with his advisers, his first step was to issue an edict in 1462 giving the trade fair held at Lyon supremacy over the one held in Geneva, which at the time was attracting more commerce. In November 1466, Louis decided to establish a royal factory for making cloth of gold in Lyon, and he offered a reduction in tithes and taxes as an inducement to lure Italian master craftsmen and weavers skilled "both in weaving said silk, and in dyeing it and other matters related to it, who will come and settle in the said place of Lyon, to carry out and exercise said work." In his efforts to attract Italian weavers, the king levied a highly unpopular tax of two thousand pounds on the Lyon silk-trading community, which, naturally, was paid with "deliberate lack of speed." The Lyon silk merchants had enjoyed a monopoly over trade in the finished fabric since 1450. Many Italian merchants made their fortunes in Lyon, and almost all major European banking houses had branches in the city. In 1466, the Medicis even moved the Geneva branch of their bank to Lyon. The reluctance of the municipal leaders to underwrite the establishment of Italian weavers and tailors in their city is therefore understandable, since it threatened to eliminate the need for their services as commercial middlemen between France and silk-rich Italy. Italian weavers who responded to the French king's call thus found themselves thwarted by the local authorities, who prevented them from establishing their workshops in the city.

Louis XI was infuriated by local hostility to his plans, and on 12 March 1469 he ordered the Lyon officials to "lead and conduct to our said city of Tours, the workers of said craft, with their mills, looms, boilers and other necessary objects." The wealthy merchants of Lyon were thus forced, despite themselves, to subsidize the first royal silk factory on French soil, by paying for the weavers' move to Tours.

The king chose Tours because his official residence was the castle at nearby Plessis-lès-Tours, and he was eager to develop the region's economy. The arrival of the Italian weavers from Lucca, via Lyon, with their draw-looms, finally made it possible for France to produce the fine, voluminous figured silks traded on the Silk Road. Although looms already existed in cities such as Avignon, they were suitable only for weaving plain velvet. Even the semi-mechanical "Jean le Calabrais" loom, common in France since the previous century, could only produce narrow pieces of figured fabric with relatively simple patterns. Meanwhile, sericulture developed throughout the Touraine region, and silk production swiftly expanded to include a greater variety of fabrics, such as velvets, satins, and damasks. The Italian influence remained, however, extremely strong.

Louis XI's successors continued his policy of developing the French silk industry and curtailing the importation of luxury goods from abroad. During his campaign in Italy, Louis XI's son Charles VIII was struck by the economic importance of the country's textile industry, and immediately implemented a number of protectionist measures in France designed to favor the weavers in Tours, and to attract more Italian weavers to Lyon. In an edict issued in 1495, he banned all cloths of gold, silver, and silk "except for those bearing the seal of a French City."

Brocatelle. France, sixteenth century. Georges Le Manach archives, Tours. Red silk and yellow linen, pattern of flowerets with royal diadem. The patterns are formed by the texture of the silk sateen weft contrasted with the linen warp. Brocatelle is characterized by the contrast between the two types of yarn used, for the warp and weft of the weave.

Right:
Brocatelle. Sixteenth century. Georges Le Manach archives, Tours.

The Reign of François I

The reign of François I (1515–47), a period of dramatic development in the arts, also witnessed the first real success of the French silk industry, which blossomed under a shower of royal commissions. François I was not content merely to continue the policies of his predecessors, but was determined to destroy the textile economy of Genoa, a city which had given its allegiance to his chief rival, Holy Roman Emperor Charles V. In any case, growth in French production became imperative in order to meet the demand for luxury goods of an opulent court yearning to emulate the magnificent silks worn by the princes and nobles of Italy. This yearning for luxury was shared by newly rich French merchants, and by a fledgling bourgeoisie attempting to imitate the nobles of the court. An Italian ambassador traveling in France at the time reported that he saw more silk there than in Constantinople and the entire Levant.

François I continued to support the silk industry in Tours, but in 1536 he also issued an edict inviting foreign weavers to settle with their families in Lyon, or in any other French city already manufacturing silk fabrics, such as Paris, Avignon, Tours, and Nîmes, in order to "make silken cloths of gold and silver, velvet, satin, and damask." He lured them with the promise that in France they would be allowed to accumulate all the goods "that they might wish, as if they were natives of this kingdom," and he also, of course, exempted them from all tithes and taxes. His hope was that these highly skilled Italian craftsmen would pass their knowledge on to French weavers, who could then gradually compete with the Italian silk industry, and especially with the famed and costly velvets from Genoa. Historians are unanimous in reporting that the first Genoese weavers to settle in Lyon were Étienne Turquet and Paule Nariz, who brought eight artisans with them and reaped all the benefits promised by the French king. The silk weavers of Tours were at the time producing the finest silks in the kingdom which they supplied to the luxury-loving court. Thibaut le Pleigney wrote in 1541: "There is no city in Christendom today where as much silken cloth is made as in the city and outskirts of Tours." The city's specialty was a heavy, durable taffeta known as *gros de Tours*. According to Venetian ambassador Marino Cavalli, in 1546 Tours contained eight thousand looms—a figure not equaled by Lyon until a century later.

Jean Clouet, *François I of France*. 1525–1530. Musée du Louvre, Paris. The rise of portraiture in the Renaissance reflected renewed focus on the individual. Kings, nobles, members of the new bourgeoisie, merchants, and women famed for their beauty commissioned portraits of themselves dressed in their most elaborate finery. Here we see a slashed doublet in figured silk, with two-tone red velvet serving as a background for the cloak's ample sleeves.

Right: Ciselé velvet produced in France *circa* 1550, most probably in Tours, which at the time boasted over eight thousand silk looms. Georges Le Manach archives, Tours.

In response to the success of the Tours silk industry, the city leaders of Lyon began to temper their hostility towards the Italian weavers. The king was anxious to see Lyon develop as a silk-weaving center, and to this end he declared it the "sole depository for all unwoven and woven silks entering the kingdom." As a result, silk grown in Spain, Italy, and the Middle East was sent directly from the port of Marseille to the custom house in Lyon.

It was now the turn of the authorities in Tours to complain of the royal privileges extended to Lyon. An especially bitter pill to swallow was the fact that their own silks now had to be sent to Lyon to receive the official customs seal before being delivered to traders. In 1554, the city fathers of Tours addressed a formal petition to the king, in which they claimed that "foreign merchants in said city (Lyon) wish to eliminate the manufacture of silk cloth in this city of Tours." This complaint was unjustified, however, since there were over eight thousand looms in Tours and its environs, and the king had decided several years previously to establish two open fairs per year, "during which merchants would be free to purchase all the silks needed by them."

THE FIELD OF THE CLOTH OF GOLD. No allusion to François I would be complete without reference to the magnificent display he mounted for his meeting with the English king Henry VIII, held from 7 to 24 June 1520. The French king's camp, known as the Field of the Cloth of Gold, was pitched in Flanders between Guînes and Ardres. The French sovereign, in his effort to dazzle his English guest, commissioned fabrics for the four hundred tents and pavilions from the guild of "merchants and master craftsmen in cloth of gold, silver, and silk" and from the braid-makers of Tours, cloth and trim valued at over sixteen thousand pounds. Eye-witnesses reported that around the camp "inside and out, in chambers and galleries, a gold bordered cloth was draped with other cloths of plain gold and cloths of gold and silver decorated with multicolored coats of arms and banners." Although it may have borne little comparison with the over-

whelming excesses of Tamerlane's Golden Horde at Samarkand, the Field of the Cloth of Gold nevertheless stands as a remarkable example of contemporary French technical and artistic prowess. This vast textile project was supervised by grand artillery master Galiot de Genouillac, and the scale models were executed by the painter Jean Fouquet's pupil, the manuscript illuminator Jean Bourdichon of Tours. Bourdichon worked closely with both weavers and gold-braiders in Tours; the braiders' role was especially important, since all the tent ropes were made of golden thread braided with turquoise-blue silk. The interiors of the tents were carpeted and hung with splendid cloth-of-gold-and-silk tapestries commissioned by François I from workshops in Brussels. The banner flying over the central pavilion showed Saint George slaying the dragon, a motif borrowed from the fourteenth-century tapestry of the Apocalyspe, made for the chapel of the castle at Angers. Here again, in an image floating above the plains of Flanders, we meet the Manichean symbols characteristic of patterns found along the Silk Road. This historic encounter was also the occasion for intense sartorial rivalry between the English and French factions, each attempting to the outdo the other with a show of finery. Although the alliance between Henry VIII and François I did not last—a few weeks later the English king shifted his support to Charles V—the magnificence of the scene would long remain etched on the memories of all who saw it.

The Ottoman Empire: Suleiman the Magnificent

At this pivotal period in history, three great leaders ruled the civilized world: Charles V, king of Spain, sovereign of the Netherlands, and, as Holy Roman Emperor, ruler of Austria and much of Germany; François I, king of France, allied with Venice; and Suleiman the Magnificent, who had raised the Turkish Ottoman Empire to worldwide eminence. The Ottoman capital was established at Constantinople, and the former Byzantine city thus recovered its power at the same time as commercial and intellectual supremacy had begun to shift from Asia to Europe, and from the Muslim to the Christian world.

As a result, textile design was marked anew by the cultural and artistic influences of the Silk Road. Star-pattern carpets woven in the Usak region contained motifs taken from the Sino-Mongol repertory of plants and flowers, and from late fifteenth-century Herat illuminated miniatures. The figures in these miniatures often wear clothing illustrated with scenes from Persian romances—an example being the series of ciselé velvets at the Musée Historique des Tissus, Lyon. A Chinese influence is also discernible in the decoration of the blue-and-white Iznik porcelain, such as the sixteenth-century "Abraham of Kütahya" type wares, which were produced to compete with the Chinese models so prized by the French court. It is also

Jan Gossaert (1478–1532), *A Nobleman*. Staatliche Museen, Berlin. Note the discreet luxury of the tunic with the small trimmed collar. The cloak is probably made from a brocatelle silk.

known that Suleiman himself habitually ate from Chinese blue-and-white porcelain plates.

Pattern books must have been as common at this period as they were in medieval Europe, since the same plant and floral motifs recur with only slight variations on book bindings, illuminations, silks, ceramics, carpets, and tooled leather. Carpet patterns also frequently included inscriptions taken from the Koran or, less frequently, from stanzas of Persian poetry. These were often used by painters for decorating tables, and meticulously copied versions appear in works by Holbein, Zurbarán, Velázquez, Vermeer, and the seventeenth-century French painter, Nicolas Tournier.

For their portraits, Ottoman sultans were shown dressed in magnificent caftans such as the silk velvet and gold robe worn by Mehmed II. The red ciselé velvet pattern, known as *cintamani*, is said to resemble Tamerlane's *tamga*, copied from a cattle brand used by nomads comprising three small circles between two clouds in the form of a ribbon. The wavy lines symbolize lightning and the small circles thunder, Tamerlane's adoptive emblems. This *tamga* recurs on many Asian and Anatolian carpets, and was copied for many years afterwards by the weavers of Constantinople who made the cloth for Ottoman court caftans. The same pattern appears on a gold-lamé ciselé velvet woven during the reign of Louis XV of France.

Portrait of Conte Giovanni Battista Vailetti, an early eighteenth-century portrait by the Italian painter Ghislandi, shows the subject dressed in Ottoman style. The silk of his doublet is similar to that used for the ceremonial caftan worn by one of Suleiman the Magnificent's sons. The gold brocade on a dark background is worked in a brilliant pattern of notched foliage, sprays of flowers and pomegranates, lotus flowers, and stylized rosettes. The cloak is made of gold cloth with a crescent pattern on a green background, and is also of Ottoman origin.

Brocade caftan worn by one of Suleiman the Magnificent's sons.

Right: Crimson silk backing, gold-and-silver brocaded pattern. Seventeenth century. Georges Le Manach archives, Tours. The Georges Le Manach factory in Tours eventually copied this pattern on a hand-powered Jacquard loom.

Fra Vittore Ghislandi, *Portrait of Conte Giovanni Battista Vailetti*. 1710. Gallerie dell'Accademia, Venice. The count is dressed in the Ottoman style: golden brocade on a ciselé velvet backing with foliage garland, no doubt woven in the imperial workshops of Constantinople.

Frans Pourbus, *A Woman
(Elisabeth of France)* detail .
1615. Musée des Beaux-Arts,
Valenciennes.

I n 1685, the British East India Company, which already had trading posts in Madras, Bombay, and Calcutta, attempted to establish commerce directly with China. The company's primary interest was not in silk or porcelain, but in tea, which at the time was as costly as gold. Canton was the only Chinese port open to foreigners, and in 1600 the Dutch had pioneered trade there through their prosperous East India Company, which also had branches in Malaga, Java, Ceylon, and Siam. The Spanish, meanwhile, had gained a foothold in Manila. Annually, a great Spanish galleon would set sail from Acapulco, laden with silver from the Mexican mines to be traded for merchandise shipped to Manila by Chinese junks. This trade route remained active from 1565 to 1815.

The French pirate Raveneau de Lussan, whose story we know from his recently discovered logbook, describes the Spanish galleon: "It is one of the finest ships sailing to India and is armed with forty canon. It sails every year from Acapulco, escorted by a vessel with twenty-eight canon ports, and laden with various sorts of cargo it transports to the inhabitants of the islands [Manila], who in exchange trade quantities of the fine Chinese and Japanese goods we see in Europe and, more precious still, pearls, gold dust, and gems." He goes on to explain how this galleon could be "boarded, and its immensely rich cargo captured." Raveneau de Lussan was active in the early seventeenth century, when rampant piracy in the China Sea often prevented Chinese silk from arriving safely in Lyon. The Dutch and British trade blockade also tended to prevent products originating in the Far East from reaching French ports.

Henri IV's sister Catherine,
Duchess of Bar. 1602.
Musée des Arts Décoratifs,
Paris.

The Development
of Sericulture in France

Henri IV (reigned 1589–1610) was one of the first French monarchs to encourage the development of French sericulture, with the aim of ensuring that part of the French weavers' demand for raw silk could be met domestically. He commissioned Olivier de Serres, an agricultural expert from the Vivarais region, to implement a vast program for planting white mulberry trees in France. Over sixty thousand seedlings from nurseries in the Languedoc were planted in the Tours, Beaujolais, and Orléans regions. The king even went so far as to order that mulberry trees be planted in public parks—the Tuileries Gardens alone received two thousand. Two years later, silkworm hatcheries were established in the same regions (at Chenonceaux, for example), and silkworm eggs distributed. In many areas, particu-

Right:

Louis XIV brocatelle silk.

Large raised design on plain

background. Georges Le

Manach archives, Tours.

larly the Protestant region of the Cévennes, sericulture became the major agricultural activity. However, while waiting for these initiatives to bear fruit, France was still forced to purchase Italian silks, and at great cost. Numerous royal edicts were issued limiting Italian imports in order to lessen the strain they imposed on the French treasury.

The Lyon silks of this period were inspired by Italian and Persian models. Contemporary inventories list jardinière or flowered velvets,

'Tum fronde, ramo, faſcibuſq; conditus. Se voluit, et pilæ in modum ſe contrahit.

Jean Stradon, engraving showing the interior of a French silkworm hatchery where silkworms are fed with fresh mulberry leaves. Late sixteenth century. Bibliothèque Nationale de France, Paris.

with gold and silver lamé backings copied from Venetian velvets, Persian-style satins, and chinoiserie taffetas. These were succeeded by the floral style that remained popular into the reign of Louis XV during the eighteenth century.

With the end of the Wars of Religion the Tours silk industry began to thrive, aided also by the promulgation of various protective measures in its favor. By the reign of Henri IV's son, Louis XIII (1610–1643), the king's chief advisor, Cardinal Richelieu was able to write in his *Political Testament*: "The panne velvets made in Tours are so fine we send them to Spain and other foreign countries . . . The red, violet, and dark velvets are finer than those made in Genoa, and Tours is also the only place where silk twill is made; their moire is finer than the English variety, their cloths of gold finer and less costly than those made in Italy." High praise indeed.

The civil wars which opposed Protestant and Catholic factions created serious economic crises and resulted in the flight from France of many Huguenot weavers, affecting all textile workers in both Lyon and Tours. When the Edict of Nantes, which guaranteed religious toleration to Protestants, finally re-established peace in

1598, the number of master silk weavers in Lyon rose from two hundred in 1595, to six hundred in 1621, to three thousand in 1660, with more than ten thousand active looms.

The huge costs of the foreign wars conducted by Louis XIII led to new sumptuary laws prohibiting "silk, gold, and silver fabrics, and all superfluity of dress"—to the despair of the Lyon weavers, who were "reduced to mendicity by the cessation of manufacture." As a center of the luxury trade, Lyon was particularly vulnerable to these dramatic crises, but each one was quickly followed by protectionist measures that infused new life into the local economy. The same phenomenon occurred during the reign of Louis XIV (1643–1715), when commissions from the French and foreign courts made Lyon the silk capital of the western world.

With the assistance of distinguished textile designers, Lyon weavers created a unique style free of all Italian influence. Louis XIV silks were patterned with large ornamental floral motifs, and bunches of grapes, fruit, and foliage, combined with architectural elements such as columns and temples. Although this style was somewhat theatrical and pompous, it perfectly suited the opulence of the Sun King's court.

France's cultural and artistic prestige, the initiatives taken by Louis XIV's finance

Brocatelle. Late seventeenth or early eighteenth century. French or Italian, with an obvious Ottoman influence in the floral pattern of tendrils with large stylized flowers. Musée des Arts de la Mode et du Textile (collection UCAD), Paris.

Turquoise-blue silk damask coverlet trimmed with gold. Seventeenth century. Originally from the Château d'Effiat in the Puy-de-Dôme. Blue Room, Château d'Azay-le-Rideau.

Right:
Red silk damask bed canopy embroidered with silver threads and trimmed in gold. Seventeenth century. Originally from the Château d'Effiat in the Puy-de-Dôme. Red Room, Château d'Azay-le-Rideau.

Brocaded lampas silk. 1725–30. Georges Le Manach archives, Tours. A large symmetrical composition on a yellow ground, in a pattern of fruit and foliage surrounded by lace scrolls. This type of lace silk was fashionable from about 1685 to 1730 for both clothing and furnishing.

Right:
Brocaded lampas silk. Early to mid-seventeenth century (Louis XIII). Georges Le Manach archives, Tours.

minister Jean-Baptiste Colbert to develop foreign trade, and the originality and quality of French textile design enabled Lyon to keep abreast of its foreign competitors. Colbert supported the "Great Factory" at Lyon, while also creating others such as the Gobelins and Beauvais factories for tapestry and carpets, and the Sèvres factory for ceramics and porcelain. Nevertheless, the life of a *canut* was far from easy. Artisans labored twelve hours a day in winter and eighteen in summer, in deplorable health and safety conditions similar to those of the imperial Sassanid and Byzantine factories, which at the time were operated by slave labor.

Poor working conditions inevitably led to conflict between merchant employers and their artisan employees. The wages paid by the merchants to their *canuts* were sometimes so low the workers had barely enough to eat, a state of affairs reflected in the words of Aristide Bruant's nineteenth-century protest song, "Pity the poor *canut*, who hasn't the money to cover his butt."

The Revocation of the Edict of Nantes

By 1685, the Lyon factory had begun to win international renown for its figured apparel and furnishing silks, and Tours could boast over eight thousand silk and three thousand ribbon looms. However, that same year, Louis XIV revoked the Edict of Nantes, forcing thousands of French Protestants, who feared a renewal of bloody religious conflict, to emigrate clandestinely. This massive exodus included bankers from Lyon, and self-employed tailors, designers, and weavers from Nîmes and Tours. With their departure, France lost precious skills to the rest of Europe, and particularly to England. The Protestant exodus from France during this period recalls the earlier fate of the Manichee weavers who, at the end of the third century, fled from religious persecution by the Sassanids, traveling first to Central Asia, and then to China.

Plate from a design book for Lyon silks. Seventeenth century. Bibliothèque du Musée des Arts Décoratifs, Paris.

Under the Edict of Nantes, Lyon had exported two hundred thousand pounds of silk annually to London. When it was revoked, many of the exiled French silk weavers set up their looms in London, thus destroying the English market for exports from Lyon. Through the trading posts of the British East India Company, London soon gained a monopoly over all Chinese silk arriving directly from Canton. Silk weavers working on drawlooms congregated in the Spitalfields section of the city, which became the major European market for all raw silk shipped from China.

Many of the most famous Spitalfields weavers were French exiles, such as Jacques Lemon from Tourcoing, Christophe Baudoin from the Pays de Caux, and Paulet of Nîmes—all extremely talented artists. Tours lost many of its weavers to London, as described in a contemporary report by a Tours city official: "The decline in this industry, which affects all the inhabitants of the City of Tours and the surrounding province, is due to several causes." He cites, first, the cessation of trade with foreign countries, which he illustrates with alarming figures; and then adds a description of "the poverty of the people that has forced many workers to depart for other places, particularly to England and Holland where their coreligionists have already established manufactories." Lyon, however, was less affected than Tours by the exodus of Protestant artisans since the city had never allowed Protestants to work in its silk factory. Although Lyon suffered relatively less than Tours from this exodus, the flight of Protestant capital caused a veritable economic disaster. The sudden dearth of operating funds reduced the number of active looms in the city from thirteen thousand to four thousand. This phenomenon also affected Tours, where the number of silk looms fell to one thousand two hundred, and the number of ribbon looms to sixty.

Brocaded lampas silk. Early eighteenth century. Pattern of foliage, floral sprays, and lace. Georges Le Manach archives, Tours.

It was at this point that French weavers, formerly held to strict quality standards, were given official permission to produce inexpensive varieties of silk based on cotton blends. Despite even this, Lyon silks maintained their reputation for excellence, and eventually spread throughout eighteenth-century Europe, a triumph due entirely to the energy and staying power of the city's remaining *canuts*.

SIAMESE AMBASSADORS VISIT VERSAILLES. By the end of the seventeenth century, Asia had become more familiar to Europeans, and ideas were further clarified by the ceremonial visit to Versailles of ambassadors from Siam, which took place on 1 September 1686. The occasion created a sensation. Numerous contemporary engravings show the Siamese ambassadors before the throne of Louis XIV in the château's Hall of Mirrors. "They wore pointed ceremonial hats a foot high, covered in white muslin and surrounded at the base with a wreath of very thin gold leaf. The king, at the height of his glory, wore a costume of silk brocade studded with large diamonds valued at many millions." The most precious of the ambassadors' offerings to the French king were wrapped in Persian, not Chinese, brocade. Louis XIV was inundated with gifts: no less than one thousand five hundred pieces of porcelain, mostly Chinese; Persian and Chinese carpets; Japanese kimonos; furnishings and screens; and boxes of Chinese and Japanese lacquer. The latter immediately captured the

Crimson, gold, and silver brocade. 1731. The King's bedchamber, Château de Versailles.
Pattern of large cartouches, foliage, flowers, exotic fruit, palmettes, palm trees, and baskets of flowers. Designed by Pierre Ringuet. This brocade, restored between 1960 and 1970, formed part of the first large royal commission from the eighteenth-century Lyon factory.

Right:
Detail of a fabric used for a bolster coverlet in the King's bedchamber, Versailles. Tassinari et Chatel archives, Paris.

imagination of the wealthy, creating a new fashion that lasted well into the eighteenth century.

In return, Louis XIV sent a French ambassadorial mission to the King of Siam bearing numerous gifts: "A golden crown set with diamonds, rubies, emeralds, and pearls; Sèvres porcelain; Savonnerie carpets, and Gobelins tapestries." The visit is recorded in several extremely picturesque documents showing the French ambassador and his escorts, dressed in their wigs and lace trimmings, arriving at the Siamese king's palace by elephant.

Hyacinthe Rigaud, *Gaspard de Gueidan Playing Music.* 1735. Musée Granet, Aix-en-Provence.
Rigaud, official portraitist to Louis XIV and Louis XV, painted a great number of his era's most eminent figures. His skillful rendering of silk drapery was learned from Flemish models.

The eighteenth century witnessed a dramatic growth in the European silk-weaving industry, reflected by the prosperity both of Spitalfields, the district in London's East End where many weavers settled, and of the French city of Lyon. Between 1720 and 1760, there were over fourteen thousand active looms in Lyon, and some thirty thousand people were employed in the manufacture of silk cloth. Spinning, dyeing, and weaving workshops burst the bounds of the city and spilled out into surrounding villages.

The humid climate in the region surrounding Lyon made it unsuitable for raising silkworms, but the city's long experience as a commercial hub compensated for this disadvantage and prepared it for a leading economic role as the capital of the silk trade. The Lyon factory gradually built up a viable infrastructure to manufacture what was to become its specialty: patterned woven silks.

These fabrics were woven on draw-looms requiring at least two workers for their operation: a weaver, and a string-puller, who stood beside the loom pulling on strings attached to ropes that controlled the yarns forming the pattern. Many experiments were conducted in an effort to simplify this process. In 1747, Vancauson built the first mechanical loom for weaving solid-color fabrics. This invention was later to inspire Joseph Marie Jacquard, who himself had worked since childhood as a string-puller. Lyon also expanded its pool of skilled workers by supporting the training of textile designers.

Unfinished embroidered white
satin bed canopy. Late
seventeenth or early
eighteenth century.
The "Filley de la Barre" bed.
Château d'Azay-le-Rideau.

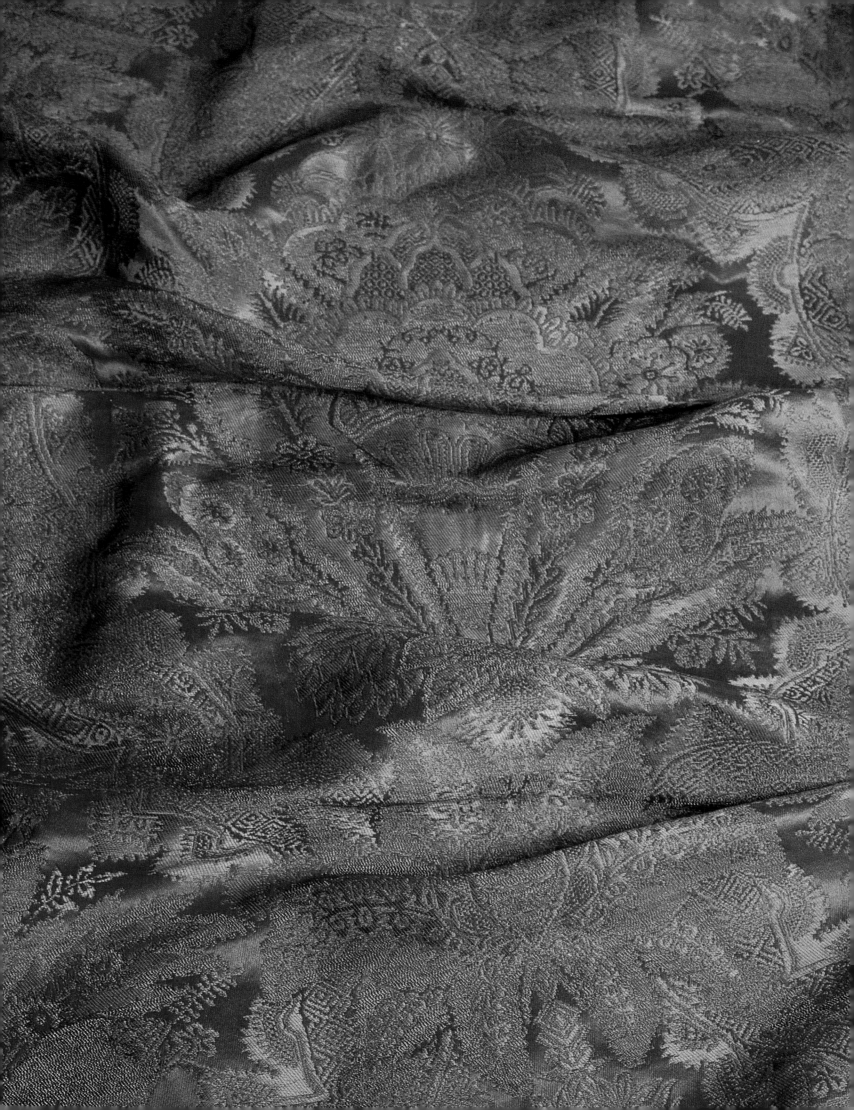

Brocaded lampas silk.
1730–40. Ratti archives,
Como (Italy).
This silk, which is probably
French, combines the natural
and artificial motifs that were
highly popular in the
mid-eighteenth century. The
vase in the shape of a bird
recalls the rococo-style silks.

Eighteenth-century silk patterns were primarily floral. Lyon silk manufacturers regularly sent their designers to Paris to meet with artists specializing in flower painting, and to visit the botanical gardens. Visits to the capital also provided an opportunity to learn about the very latest fashions in clothing and furniture. In a further effort to support local design, the members of the Académie de Lyon founded a free school in January 1757 which offered courses in painting, sculpture, geometry, and botany.

Textile designers studied loom techniques so they could adapt their patterns to make the most of available technology. In 1733, Jean Revel perfected the *point rentré* technique, in which weft threads of different colors are used to create subtle, realistic effects. Philippe de Lasalle invented a process of interchangeable loom "simples" for executing oversize patterns. The simple is a manually-set program which the puller can use to raise all the warp threads simultaneously in order to execute the pattern. Prior to this technical innovation, oversize designs could only be made by sewing together two pieces of fabric, each containing a separate component of the pattern.

Waistcoat. *c.* 1735–45.
Musée de la Mode et du
Costume, Paris.

The Evolution of Textile Decoration

Over the course of the eighteenth-century, textile patterns began to reflect the taste for exoticism that had developed in France during the reign of Louis XV. A new silk pattern, referred to as "bizarre," made its appearance between 1695 and 1710. Bizarre silks were woven with semi-abstract designs containing fragmentary architectural motifs combined with plants and animals in asymmetrical compositions. Bizarre patterns featured vividly colored backgrounds and were often brocaded in gold or silver thread. These designs were influenced by goods imported from the Far East—lacquer, porcelain, silk, and cotton fabrics—and they exemplified the contemporary taste for art from distant and as yet mysterious lands. A panel containing

Left:

Lampas silk. Eighteenth century (Louis XV). Georges Le Manach archives, Tours.

Large-patterned silk. Late seventeenth or early eighteenth century. Georges Le Manach archives, Tours. An ornamental bizarre silk recognizable by the semi-abstract motifs based on oriental models.

the *Second Chinese Suite*, woven at Beauvais from cartoons painted by François Boucher in 1742, shows an evolution in the chinoiserie style toward greater freedom of interpretation. Imaginative oriental human figures, pagodas, and fabulous flowers were the major characteristics of this type of decoration and a major component of the rococo style which developed during the reign of Louis XV and influenced all the decorative arts. Louis XV's celebrated favorite, Madame de Pompadour, was a shareholder in the French East India Company and gave considerable impetus to this fashion by commissioning fabrics with chinoiserie motifs from Lyon designers, including, among many others, Jean Pillement.

In the early eighteenth century, another textile style featuring lacy scrolls framing flowers, fruits, and stylized palmettes became increasingly popular. The best examples of this lace silk date from the 1720s.

During the next decade, from 1730 to 1740, a turning point in textile design occurred. New experiments for creating an illusion of depth produced patterns that were more realistic, a trend consistent with changing eighteenth-century tastes. Large floral motifs were worked in all-over patterns, sometimes horizontally. From 1740 to 1750, architectural elements, exotic human figures, and even musical motifs were added. From 1745 to 1760 fabric patterns adopted a vertical disposition, and

featured realistic flowers in greatly reduced numbers, arranged in superimposed bouquets framed with ribbon-scrolls of imitation white lace, or in wavy garlands sometimes decorated with feathers. In 1760, vertical stripes of various widths were added.

In around 1775, fabric patterns evolved once more, this time into extremely delicate, perfectly balanced floral motifs, sometimes including narrow stripes, and often trimmed with rows of pearls, tufted fringes, or slender ribbons. Lightweight apparel fabrics gained in popularity and, in the late eighteenth century, clothing-fabric patterns tended to be miniaturized. Conversely, furnishing fabrics—frequently commissioned by royalty—were woven in increasingly large patterns. Designer Philippe de Lasalle was responsible for a number of floral and animal motifs in vibrantly colored, balanced

Cushion with ornamental trimming. Rubelli archives, Venice.

Brocaded lampas silk. Eighteenth century (Louis XV). Georges Le Manach archives, Tours.

Right:
Brocaded lampas silk. Eighteenth century (Louis XV). Rococo design of realistic flowers and lambrequins. Georges Le Manach archives, Tours.

The Golden Age of Silk

Right:

Tapestry by Philippe de Lasalle for Catherine the Great of Russia. *c.* 1773. Brocaded lampas and chenille silk. The medallions enclose alternating pairs of peacocks and ducks, pheasants and swans. This tapestry was rewoven by Prelle and Tassinari et Chatel.

Detail of the Gaudin furnishing silk. 1788–89. Prelle archives, Lyon. Chenille silk was used increasingly often from the 1770s onwards.

compositions. Lasalle's highly detailed sketches indicate how the different yarns are to be used in order to create a pattern through contrasts in the weave: satin against taffeta or silk twill, for example. Lasalle also used lustrous silks and the new chenille yarns to create weave contrasts. The silk he designed *circa* 1773 for Catherine the Great's palace in St. Petersburg is an outstanding example of the elaborate Lasalle style. Intertwined branches frame two sets of birds: a pheasant and a swan, and a peacock and two ducks. Lasalle also designed intricate woven portraits, including a portrait of Catherine the Great probably dating from 1771, an example of which hung in Voltaire's salon at Ferney.

The most extraordinary example of eighteenth-century tapestry, however, is the "Gaudin" furnishing fabric. This brocaded white satin is patterned with large laurel-

Gaudin furnishing silk. 1788–89. Prelle archives, Lyon.

Brocaded white satin with a pattern of flowers, palm tress, birds, trophies, and pastoral scenes. Often attributed to Philippe Lasalle, this furnishing fabric was purchased by the royal household from Lyon manufacturer Gaudin in 1789. The fabric was perhaps originally intended for one of the queen's chambers. In 1805 it was placed in the Empress's bedchamber at Fontainebleau.

leaf arabesques framing birds and architectural, musical, and pastoral motifs. It was begun by Lyon weaver Gaudin then, when the latter went bankrupt, purchased by Thierry de Ville-d'Avray, General Commissioner of Royal Household Furnishings, who had the piece completed, adding embroidered fabrics for chairs and bed. The entire suite was intended for the queen's bedchamber, but it was not until the early years of the Empire that it found a final home in the bedchamber of the Empress Josephine at Fontainebleau, where it was installed in 1805. It remained there until it was rewoven in 1965 by Prelle and Tassinari et Chatel, and re-inaugurated in 1986.

White satin with embroidered silk medallion appliqués. Tassinari et Chatel archives, Paris.

This silk, designed by Gandoin, was ordered in 1779 for the winter furnishings of Marie-Antoinette's private apartments at Versailles. The panel in the photograph is a Second Empire copy (*c.* 1859) woven for the Empress Eugenie's private apartments in the Tuileries Palace. This fabric was restored by Tassinari from 1988 to 1994 for the billiard room in Marie-Antoinette's private apartments at Versailles.

At the end of the eighteenth century, furnishing fabrics woven in an antique style favored by contemporary fashion-setters became popular.

A unique design technique was developed in 1740. This was the *chiné à la branche* method, a type of resist-dyeing. By resist-dyeing the yarns used for the fabric's warp, delicately shaded outlines could be achieved for these mostly floral patterns. The subtle hazy effects of the *chiné à la branche* method were used for taffeta, *gros de Tours,* and—less often—for ciselé velvet. All of these resist-dyed fabrics were popular for both furnishing and apparel.

Left:

Brocaded *gros de Tours* in a floral and arabesque pattern. Prelle archives, Lyon. Commissioned from Desparges in 1786 for Louis XVI's bedchamber at Saint-Cloud. This silk was subsequently used to decorate Napoleon I's bedchamber at the Tuileries Palace.

Women's Fashions and Silk

During the eighteenth century, feminine fashions followed the lead of textile designers. Since clothing styles themselves changed only slightly, the fabrics from which garments were made served as the focus for shifting tastes in fashion. Although cotton began to appear as a serious rival from 1750 onwards silk remained clearly in the spotlight for most of the century.

The height of elegant fashion at the beginning of the century was the flying-panel dress, often glibly referred to as the "Watteau" dress. This voluminous, sweeping garment could be open or closed in the front, and featured the characteristic floor-length flying-panel gathered into unpressed or box pleats attached to the upper back. The dress was worn over large panniers or hoops that were at first funnel- and then bell-shaped. As the shape of the panniers changed during the 1730s, the dress became more rounded at sides and back. For the new bell-shaped skirt, the

flying-panel was gathered into a double box pleat on the upper back. This more complicated style came to be known as the *robe à la française*. The bodice of these dresses was stiffened with whalebone stays sometimes trimmed with lace and ribbon, and the skirt was generally made of the same material as the bodice. Fabrics with large floral patterns were ideal for this type of dress which, because of its ample volume, showed them off to maximum advantage. From 1730 to 1750, large patterns of luxuriant flowers accentuated the lateral extension of the dresses. The greatest era, however, for the *robe à la française* occurred between 1750 and 1765, when dress and fabric styles achieved an ideal symbiosis rarely encountered in the history of fashion. When the woman wearing the dress moved, the panniers underneath the skirt swayed from side to side, focusing attention on the vertical rhythm of the pattern.

Brocaded lampas silk. 1760. Georges Le Manach archives, Tours.

Robe à la française made
from *chiné à la branche*
taffeta. *c.* 1755–65.
Musée des Arts de la Mode
et du Textile (collection
UFAC), Paris.

Lampas silk dress with flying-
panel in back. *c.* 1730.
Musée des Arts de la Mode
et du Textile (collection
UFAC), Paris.

Robe à la française.
c. 1755–60. Musée de la Mode et du Costume, Paris. Lampas silk with S-shaped pattern in the rococo spirit that characterized mid-eighteenth-century decorative arts.

In 1760, the general cut of the *robe à la française* began to change. Bodices and waistlines became more fitted, and the pleats of the flying-panel much smaller. A new style emerged in 1780, shifting the focus from the horizontal to the vertical and simplifying both cut and fabric designs. This style, known as the *robe à l'anglaise*, featured an arched, fitted back molded by whalebone stays, and a high-waisted, gathered skirt worn over hip padding. Fabrics were patterned in stripes of various widths that emphasized the new vertical line.

As the volume of the dress decreased, fabric motifs became smaller and more delicate. This style finally evolved into the sheath or tunic dresses of the late eighteenth century. These were often made of cotton, which gained rapidly in popularity, or of lightweight silk in solid colors or miniature scatter patterns.

Patterned silk bodice.

c. 1760–70.

Fulgence collection, Paris. The meticulous matching of the pattern reflects a characteristic eighteenth-century concern for using the cut of the garment to show off the pattern.

Right:

Robe à l'anglaise.

c. 1780–85. Musée de la Mode et du Costume, Paris. Brocaded pekin in a pattern of tone-on-tone stripes. The fitted cut of this *robe à l'anglaise* and the pattern of subtle stripes reflects a trend that began in 1780 towards simpler, more vertical styles for women's dress.

Embroidery and Lace

A marked inclination, during the late eighteenth century, towards elegant simplicity in dress was also reflected in embroidery styles. Lyon became the most important European center for silk embroidery, well ahead of both London and Paris. Satin- and chain-stitch embroideries were executed to order on backing fabrics that were usually light-colored. Tailors and dressmakers then simply cut the strips of pre-sewn embroidery to fit the measurements of their clients' garments. Embroidery was used on men's waistcoats and as bodice trim for the formal dresses worn at

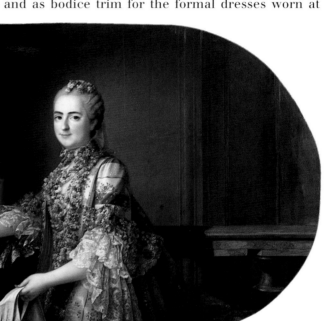

Portrait of Marie-Louise, daughter of Louis XV (left) and of Madame Sophie, daughter of Louis XV (right). Studio of François-Hubert Drouais (1727–75). Door lintel. Château de Versailles. The dresses worn by both ladies feature prominent striped patterns.

court on occasions when etiquette decreed that full court attire (whalebone stays, full skirt and train attached at the waist) could be dispensed with. Embroidery patterns were often figurative, and tended to follow current fashions for the exotic, the rustic, the heroic, and the allegorical.

Lace was an important accessory in every eighteenth-century wardrobe. Men and women alike wore lace daily, trimming their costumes with lace fichus, cravats, and *engageantes*—the detachable lace ruffles used to trim the sleeves of dresses. From 1750 onwards there was an unparalleled craze for lace, the finest examples of which were made of silk. The *blonde* variety, made from undyed silk yarn, was especially prized.

Silk purse.
Fulgence collection, Paris.

Trimmed silk. *c.* 1750–60.
Rubelli archives, Venice.

Pattern book.
Prelle archives, Lyon.

Top:

Dancing Satyr. 1797.

Lampas silk by Pernon, based

on a design by Dugourc for

the ballroom of the Casita

del Labrador in Aranguez.

Beneath: this is a

tile-patterned satin

embroidered in polychrome

silk, commissioned from

Pernon in 1808 for

Napoleon's bedchamber at

Meudon. Tassinari et Chatel

archives, Paris.

L yon recovered its predominant role as a silk-manufacturing center following the upheavals of the French Revolution, and with the dawn of the nineteenth century confidently entered the Industrial age. Extensive research was undertaken in order to improve the yield and lower the costs of silk production, with the government leading the way. Napoleon Bonaparte and his wife Josephine paid a visit to Lyon in 1802, to demonstrate their personal interest in the local industry. Between 1802 and 1808, Bonaparte commissioned a quantity of fabrics for the imperial palaces at the Tuileries, Fontainebleau, and Versailles. In 1805, he encouraged Joseph Marie Jacquard, inventor of the Jacquard loom, by granting him fifty francs for every loom put into operation using his new system. By devising a method for automating the traditional draw-loom, Jacquard had pioneered the most dramatic revolution in the history of the Silk Road. Born on 7 July 1752, he grew up during the reign of Louis XV, spent his young manhood under Louis XVI and ended his days on 7 April 1834, when Louis Philippe was on the throne. Jacquard's father was a master weaver specializing in gold-brocaded silk, and the son first met designer Philippe de Lasalle in the paternal workrooms. His mother was a pattern-card reader, and he was profoundly influenced by the sight of the looms' string-pullers—usually women and children—living out their entire lives, in the words of one Abbé Vassart, "In strained, unnatural postures more than prejudicial to the healthy development of life and limb, braced against excessively heavy bundles of ropes . . . There is a heart-rending contrast, as if to illustrate fate's perpetual irony, between the richness of the fabrics and the poverty of the workers; the brilliant colors of the cloth and the grim darkness of the workrooms." Jacquard's invention was based on a number of technical advances made during the previous century. Applying the principle of perforated cards to loom programming, he invented a device with which a single worker could weave the

most complicated patterns. The accuracy of the pattern replication was so great using this technique that copies of paintings by romantic artists could be—and were—reproduced on black and white woven silk. A card-reader developed by Berly in 1818 made it possible to perforate all the holes for a single card simultaneously, thus facilitating the transcription of designs still further. This additional invention contributed significantly to the spread of the Jacquard loom, increasing the yield and thus lowering the cost for woven patterned fabrics. The weavers themselves were less than enthusiastic, however, complaining that the new looms would ruin the Lyon silk industry and put the city's women and children out of work. As a result, early Jacquard looms were often the victims of sabotage on the part of workers attempting to discredit the new invention. Looms would mysteriously break down and, when Jacquard was called in to inspect them, just as mysteriously begin to work again.

An eye-witness report of workers' resistance to the Jacquard loom penned by Jean-François Grognier has survived: "As early as 1804, the model loom that had been sent to the Palace of the Arts was removed and burned on the Place des Terreaux. Several workroom supervisors took apart the Jacquard looms that had been given to them by their employers and sold the components as scrap iron, rope, and wood. The workers with the strongest grievance against the new machines were, of course, the pattern foremen, those tyrants of the workroom who ruled their weavers, rope- and string-pullers, card-readers, and loom fitters with absolute despotism. Foremen's wages were generous compared with those of their

Camille Pernon, green damask in palm tree pattern with a border of gold brocade on a poppy-red ground. 1802–05. Tassinari et Chatel archives, Paris.
This silk was woven for the First Consul's library in the Château de Saint-Cloud (later to become Napoleon's study).

Right:
Camille Pernon, silver and blue brocade with wreaths of myrtle and ivy. 1802–05. This furnishing fabric was commissioned for Josephine Bonaparte's grand salon at Saint-Cloud as part of Napoleon's effort to support the Lyon silk industry.

underlings, and they could never forgive the machine that had put an end to their minor aristocracy." The industrial era was at hand, and with it came bitter social struggle. In about 1830, manufacturers went north of the Loire river in search of more docile peasant laborers. In vain, however, since the response to this strategy was the great uprising of the Lyon *canuts* in November 1831. On 13 March 1834, just a few months before Jacquard died, Lamartine gave a lengthy speech to the French Chamber of Deputies in which he alluded with passion to the Lyon insurrection:

"I deplore the blood that has been shed, and the violation of public order, and the attack on the public economy in the second-ranking city of the kingdom. But I especially deplore the initial and dangerous symptoms of a social ill that has long been in the making, and the excessive expansion of an industry that gathers huge numbers of people into a single trade which may suddenly fail them."

However, despite all the opposition to Jacquard, by 1826 there were thirty thousand looms operating in Lyon, four thousand of them equipped with his device.

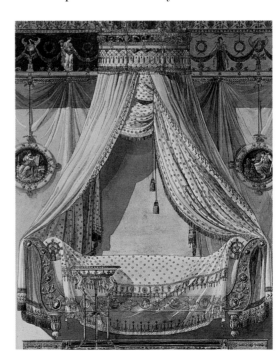

AMYNTHE DÉLIVRE SYLVIE.   FRANCOIS BOUCHER.

Other Technical Improvements

As technical advances continued to be made in reeling, and especially in dyeing, new research began to focus on diversifying the ways in which the finished fabrics could be used. In 1808, Napoleon ordered the establishment of an industrial chemistry course in Lyon, and in 1810 he offered an award to encourage the discovery of a substitute for the over-expensive indigo dye. In 1811, the award was won by Jean-Michel Raymond, whose blue potassium ferrocyanide dye also earned him a gold medal at an exhibition of industrial arts held in 1819. Research continued throughout the nineteenth century, eventually resulting in the invention of fuchsin (a magenta-colored dye) and the development of the piece-dyeing process. The use of steam in the silk industry, pioneered by Gensoul in 1823, improved the quality of

Camille Pernon, gold brocade with a jonquil-yellow and blue design in Turkish-style motifs. Lyon, 1802–05. Commissioned for Josephine Bonaparte's bedchamber at Saint-Cloud and actually used in 1808–09 for Empress Marie-Louise's bedchamber at Compiègne, which in 1811 became her son, the king of Rome's nursery.

Right:
Napoleon's bedchamber at Compiègne. Furniture seats, backs, and sides in crimson damask with a mosaic design of oak leaves, stars, and bees. Front and side edging panels in crimson silk damask with a design of palms, stars, rushes, and foliage. Wall hangings, bed canopy and curtains in the same damask as that used for the furniture. Originally woven by Camille Pernon of Lyon in 1806. Rewoven by Tassinari et Chatel in 1976.

silk yarn and led to the introduction of large-scale reeling factories. French silk production still failed to meet domestic demand, however, especially during the latter part of the century when silkworms were decimated by disease. Weavers in Tours and Lyon were forced to import raw silk from across the Mediterranean: bales of silk were sent from Beirut to Marseille on the ships of the Imperial French merchant fleet, then on to Lyon by river. In 1858, France signed a trade agreement with China establishing a direct route from Canton to Marseille. In the second half of the nineteenth century, fifty percent of the raw silk processed in Lyon came from China. The inauguration of the Suez Canal in 1869 finally opened a direct sea route between East and West.

Meanwhile, in order to satisfy increasing demand for less expensive fabrics, Lyon manufacturers began to blend their silk with wool or cotton. Research into the possibility of creating an artificial silk bore fruit in work by Count Hilaire de Chardonnet, who registered a patent in 1884 for a silky chemical fiber made from a blend of cellulose and cotton linters.

Damask drapes with lampas silk border. François I salon at Fontainebleau. Not hung until the Second Empire (1856).

Right:
Chiné velvet patterned with sprays of fruit, laurel leaves, and flowers. Woven by Grand Frères (1811–13), but not installed until 1858. Armchair attributed to Jacob Frères; couch by Jacob Desmalter (1806). Emperor's bedchamber, Fontainebleau.

The Lyon Factory

During the first half of the nineteenth century, the Lyon factory depended to a great extent on the substantial commissions it received from official government circles. As the century wore on, however, it began to serve the needs of the emerging bourgeoisie, and also added wealthy Americans to its list of foreign clients. By about 1850, sixty percent of the city's production was being exported to the major royal courts and cities of Europe, and also to America. Although Lyon continued to manufacture luxury patterned silks (most frequently commissioned, after 1860, by the emerging *haute couture* houses), it also met mass consumer demand for solid-color fabrics, lightweight crepes and tulles, inexpensive silk muslins, and, especially, the new, less expensive blends.

Lyon won international renown through the participation of its silk weavers in various World's Fairs, and the city's leading firms began to form the voluminous archives that today serve as priceless sources of iconographical data, gathering them in the Musée d'Art et d'Industrie (founded in 1864), which was later to become the Musée Historique des Tissus.

During Napoleon's rule as emperor of France (1804–14), restoration work began on the palaces ravaged by the French Revolution, leading to major official commissions for fabrics. In 1806, six tapestries were ordered for Versailles from Camille Pernon, former purveyor to the royal household who was eventually succeeded by Grand Frères. Only one of the tapestries was installed immediately, however. This

Two-ply brocatelle based on a
design by Charles Garnier,
woven in 1874 for the foyer
of the Paris Opera.
Prelle archives, Lyon.

Right:
Copper-plate and metallic
lampas silk brocade with a
twill background, used *circa*
1819 for Louis XVIII's Council
Chamber at the Tuileries
palace. Prelle archives, Lyon.

CHUARD·ET·Cᵉ   A·LYON·1819

Camille Pernon et Grand Frères pattern book (July 1856 to May 1870). Tassinari et Chatel archives, Paris.

was the crimson satin embroidered with oak and laurel leaves framed by palm trees that went to the throne room. In 1810, around ninety thousand yards of solid-color and patterned fabrics were commissioned for Versailles, of which over seventy-five thousand yards still had not been used when the Empire ended. This commission included brocades, velvets, *gros de Tours*, gold- and silver-embroidered silks, lampas, and damask in various shades of green, blue, yellow, and crimson. Most of the patterns were based on the emblematic laurels, oak leaves, and bees associated with Napoleon, but naturalistic floral motifs were also frequent, as in the matched white satin and silk with wreaths of daisies and bouquets of roses executed between 1811 and 1815 for the empress's bedchamber at Versailles.

Sample book. Georges Le Manach archives, Tours.

Silk swatches. Rubelli archives, Venice.

These fabrics initiated a new style featuring imposing and complicated patterns that were nevertheless meticulously arranged and framed by medallions, lozenges, and fine latticework.

During the period of the Bourbon Restoration (1815–1830), the Lyon factory received a number of major commissions from the royal household, including hangings for the bedchamber of Louis XVIII, and the summer furnishing fabrics for the throne room in the Tuileries. Ordered in 1817 from Grand Frères and designed by Saint-

Right:
Samples of furnishing trim from the Passementerie Nouvelle archives, Paris. Various examples of silk-and-gold threaded tassels.

All-over two-ply lampas silk
with shaded brocading from a
design by Beuchot, woven for
the Hôtel Cail.
Prelle archives, Lyon.

Ciselé velvet, gold-lamé
background, commissioned
by the Vanderbilts in 1890 for
re-upholstering the dining
room chairs at Marble House.
Prelle archives, Lyon.

Right:
Two-ply lampas silk woven in
1871 for Prince Pogzeboff.
Design by Vigoureux.
Prelle archives, Lyon.

Pattern book from the
archives of Jean Roze, Tours.

Woven-silk bookmark commemorating one hundred years of silk manufacture in the city of Macclesfield. Great Britain, 1896. Collection of the Macclesfield Museums Trust.

Ange, the hangings for the bedchamber constituted the first major official commission for which Raymond's chemical blue was used. This sustained blue, combined with the optical illusion of depth provided by the ciselé velvet, created a unique effect that has since come to be associated with the French Restoration period. The summer furnishing fabrics for the throne room, also commissioned from Grand Frères but this time based on designs by the famous Jean Démosthène Dugoure, are exceptionally fine and epitomize the taste for heavily draped interiors characteristic of the period.

Although official commissions declined as the century advanced, they were replaced by the patronage of wealthy individuals such as Jacques Lafitte, who in 1823 ordered the furnishing fabrics for his Parisian town house from Grand Frères.

The new style in furnishing fabrics became more entrenched by mid-century, in step with the nascent taste for over-stuffed upholstery. Succulent fruits and flowers were depicted naturalistically amid leafy scrolls and clouds. In 1860, tastes shifted again, this time restoring to favor the delicate patterns of floral tendrils, ribbon streamers, and baskets of the late eighteenth century, as was evident from many of the textiles presented at the 1889 Paris World's Fair. The year 1889 also marked a renewal in the decorative skills of Lyon designers. Although both naturalistic and stylized flowers retained their popularity, they were no longer diluted in broad and diffuse compositions, but set off from their backgrounds in dramatic designs which highlighted their intrinsic decorative power. This shift in fabric styles was hastened by new demands from the world of clothing fashion, which in simplifying the feminine silhouette had once again focused interest on the patterns of dress fabrics.

Right:
A large French drapers' establishment at the time of the Second Empire (1848–1870). Roger-Viollet, Paris.

Indiscret settee, characteristic of the over-stuffed style prevalent during the second half of the nineteenth century. Napoleon III salon, Château de Compiègne.

Silk and Fashions in Clothing

In the course of the nineteenth century, silk yielded its place as the standard fabric for men's clothing to wool. For women's clothing, however, it continued to hold its own, despite strong competition from cotton. Where in the eighteenth century, fabric and fabric patterns had served as much, if not more than the design of the garment itself as the focus of visual interest, in the new century clothing styles—especially for women—began to change at the accelerated pace we now associate with "fashion," and this naturally had an impact on fabric design. Unwieldy crinolines and bustles (which do not move with the same rhythmic sway as eighteenth-century panniers), a taste for contrasting textures, such as velvet with satin, and the

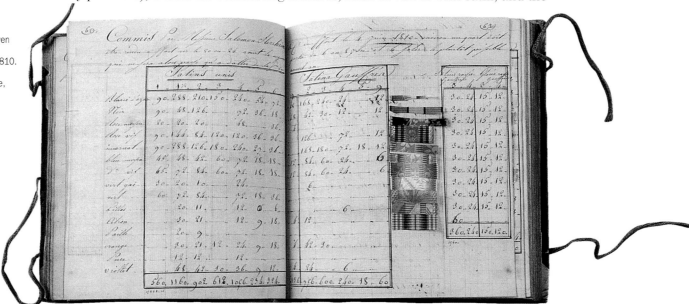

importance of lace, ribbon, braid, embroidery, and jet-bead trimming all worked against the use of large patterns, which lose their effect when stifled by elaborate drapery and accessories.

The women of the emerging nineteenth-century bourgeoisie became major customers for high fashion as they strove for social recognition by (among other things) emulating the tastes of a confirmed aristocracy who believed elegance lay in simplicity. A further factor in changing fabric styles was the demand for clothing silks stimulated by the new department stores that devoted whole counters and sometimes whole floors to selling silk. Manufacturers responded to this new market by producing affordable fabrics—often blends—in simple patterns.

Left:

Jean-Auguste-Dominique
Ingres, *Portrait of the
Princesse de Broglie*. 1853.
Metropolitan Museum of Art
(Lehman collection),
New York.

Following pages:

Tea gown. *c.* 1865–70.
Owned by Princess Mathilde.
Château de Compiègne.

Silk taffeta ball gown.
1850–55. Musée de la Mode
et du Costume, Paris.

Worth's career began in 1853 when he joined the famed Gagelin department store as an assistant, later rising to become a partner in the business. In 1858 he formed a partnership with Gustave Bobergh and opened his own couture house on the rue de la Paix in Paris. Bobergh retired in 1870, leaving Worth in sole charge of the firm. As a designer, Worth specialized in ball dresses and court presentation gowns, spearheading such innovations as wisps of silk tulle draped over satin or taffeta for a gauzy-cloud effect. This type of dress can been seen in portraits of high-society ladies by Franz Xavier Winterhalter, such as that of the Empress Elizabeth of Austria painted in 1865.

Evening dress by Lafferière.
c. 1883. Silk, duchesse
satin, and damask.
Underskirt in cotton muslin.
This elaborate style called for
near-solid silks and
contrasting textures.
Musée de la Mode et du
Costume, Paris.

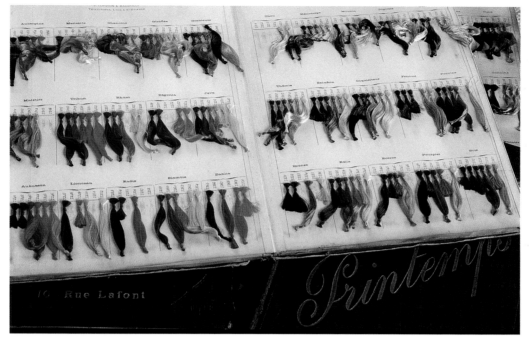

In the years preceding the fall of Napoleon III and the end of the Second Empire in 1870, the silks used by Worth were similar to those used by his contemporaries. Patterns remained relatively simple, serving as foils for elaborate trim. Finally, towards the late 1880s, large-patterned fabrics became one of Worth's "signatures." At this point dresses had become more vertical, and skirts worn over padding, crinolines, or bustles were flattened at the waist and hips in order to highlight the pattern of the fabric. Worth and his sons, who succeeded him in 1895, were eager to support the Lyon silk weavers. In 1889, Worth designed a ball dress using a silk brocade with a pattern of Dutch tulips on a black ground that had just been exhibited at the World's Fair by the Lyon firm of Gourd. The difficulties involved in weaving this fabric, which required a total of thirty-one thousand pattern cards on a mechanical Jacquard loom, earned a princely sum for its manufacturer. Other silks with large floral patterns presented at the Lyon World's Fair in 1894 were also used by Worth, and today these remain emblematic of the close bonds forged at an early stage between French *haute couture* and the silk weavers of Lyon.

T oday, silk accounts for only .2 percent of textile fiber production worldwide, an extremely small quantity which reflects the relative weakness of this commodity—but also its strength. Silk is rare and highly prized, a fabric synonymous with technical innovation and luxury.

The members of the International Silk Association, founded in 1949, include all the countries that produce or consume this unique material. The association supervises and regulates the international silk trade, sponsors scientific research, and initiates promotional campaigns. It also protects the official "silk" label distinguishing this natural yarn from the host of chemical substitutes that have been developed in modern times. Also, as explained by the association's secretary general Ronald Currie, the overall term *soierie,* or silk-type, is applicable to any fiber woven with the same equipment and according to the same techniques as pure silk.

The phenomenal development of chemical yarns in the twentieth century has made it possible to meet the continuously expanding clothing industry's demand for low-cost products. The Lyon silk industry has responded to this evolution by bringing its advanced technical skills, flexibility, and capacity for change to the manufacture and improvement of fabrics made with the new yarns.

Chemical yarns fall into two basic categories: artificial yarns made from cellulose, and synthetics. The first artificial yarns were developed in the 1880s by Count Hilaire de Chardonnet, who used cotton linters to produce nitrocellulose rayon. Bemberg, or cuprammonium stretch rayon, developed in the early twentieth century, was followed by rayon viscose, which is used extensively for both clothing and furnishing

fabrics. By 1926, Lyon weavers were producing almost as much artificial fabric as silk, and in 1930 spun rayon was added to their repertory.

Synthetic yarns, which first appeared during the 1930s, are the culmination of intensive research aimed at discovering methods for creating man-made yarns with chemical properties similar to those found in nature. They are made from organic substances, such as petroleum derivatives and castor oil, and can be divided into four basic types: polyamides, polyesters, vinyls, and acrylics. In 1938, the American chemical giant Du Pont de Nemours launched the first genuine synthetic yarn, which was given the generic name Nylon. A further revolution overtook the clothing industry in 1959 when the same company introduced the elastomer yarn Lycra, from which today's stretch fabrics are made.

In 1993, the Lyon region produced 70,714 metric tons of cloth from raw materials that included (among others) 362 tons of silk, 9,154 tons of artificial yarn, and 24,021 tons of synthetic yarns. Of the 240 silk-fabric weavers currently operating in Lyon and the surrounding region, only four work with pure silk alone and less than fifteen work with silk more than eighty percent of the time. These statistics provide eloquent proof of the fundamental changes that have occurred in the silk industry. Since silk weaving is a highly complicated process, silk looms have proved ideal for experimenting with artificial and synthetic yarns. However, due to their inherent properties and to the mass-production methods involved in their manufacture, the new yarns have come primarily to be used to meet the demands of a mass consumer market.

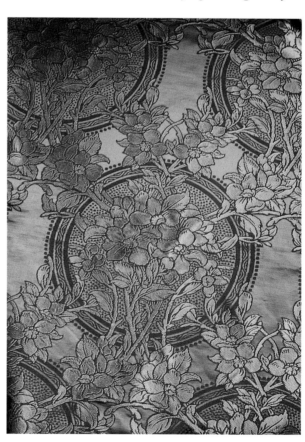

Progress in Loom Technology

One of the major twentieth-century innovations in the field of weaving was the development of automatic and shuttle looms. Because they can be operated at high speeds, these looms increase productivity yet require a smaller work force. The old mechanical shuttle or "pick-and-pick" looms have gradually been replaced by automatic quill-changing looms, on which the weft yarn can be replaced without stopping the loom. On ordinary automatic looms the weft yarn is propelled by a jet of water or compressed air; and on rapier looms by a semi-rigid ribbon attached to a clip. Mechanical looms are, however, still used for particularly complicated weaves—the reproductions of historic furnishing fabrics woven for the restoration of French châteaux, for example, which are executed on handlooms, the only type capable of duplicating the elaborate brocade patterns of the past. Firms such as Quenin-Lelièvre, Prelle, and Tassinari et Chatel still run traditional handlooms, and remain faithful to the venerable traditions of the Lyon silk industry.

Three decisive new factors have marked the history of silk in the twentieth century: the increased use of silk blended with other materials, the popularity of silk prints, and the recent proliferation of washed silk. Research begun early in the century has focused on ways to blend silk with other materials: with synthetics, to lower its cost; with luxury yarns such as mohair and cashmere for variety; and with Lycra, for producing the ultra-modern stretch silk.

In 1925, the screen printing process was developed in Lyon, resulting in the decline of woven patterns. For silk screen printing, the proposed pattern is outlined on a piece of permeable silk gauze (the screen), which is then stretched over a rigid frame. Separate screens are used for each color in the pattern, and are lowered successively onto a piece of fabric stretched over a table. Once the screen is in place, it is covered with dye using a squeegee, which presses the color through the unblocked portions of the gauze onto the fabric beneath. The fabric is allowed to dry and the process is then repeated until all the colors have been applied and the entire pattern reproduced. As many colors as desired can be applied, using different screens, which makes silk screen printing ideal for the reproduction of subtle nuances in shading.

Gold-brocade lampas silk by Suzanne Lalique. Woven in 1914 by Tassinari et Chatel. Tassinari et Chatel archives, Paris.

Insects, by Paul Follot. Woven in 1910 by Tassinari et Chatel. Tassinari et Chatel archives, Paris.

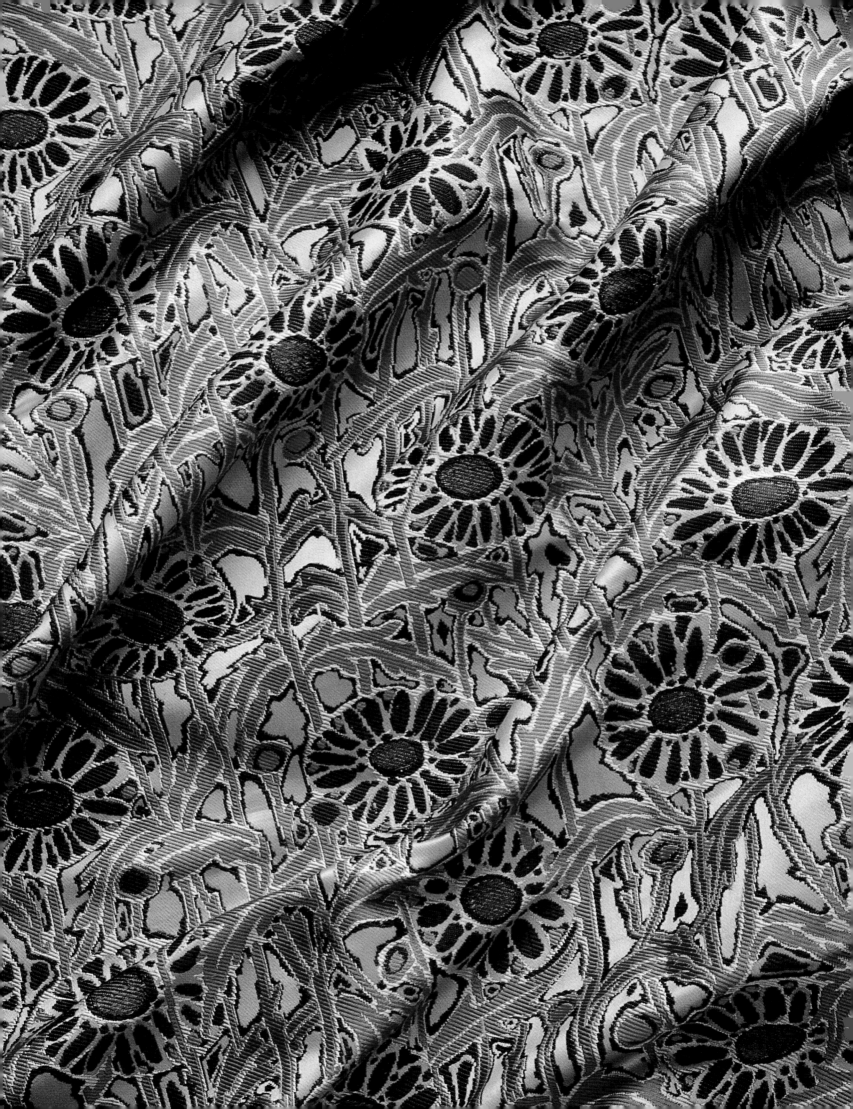

Mariano Fortuny y Madrazo

Mariano Fortuny, the "Delphos" robe in pleated silk taffeta.

Mariano Fortuny y Madrazo was born in Grenada to a family of artists. An innate curiosity fueled his interest in a diversity of fields including painting, engraving, and photography, and the design of stage sets, fabrics, and clothing. Like William Morris, Fortuny believed artists should exercise total control over every aspect of their creation, and he was endlessly intrigued by technical innovations which made it possible to put his theories into practice. He set up his print workshop in Venice's Palazzo Orfei, where he worked almost exclusively with unbleached and bleached silk which he dyed, printed, embossed, and pleated. Fortuny sought out fabrics that would cling to the natural contours of the body, and he used the lightest of silk velvets for coats, capes, and dresses; silk sateen and pongee for pleated dresses; and silk voile and gauze for gossamer tunics. In about 1907, he chose finely pleated silk pongee for his famous "Delphos" robe, named in honor of the Auriga statue at Delphi. The Delphos model consists of a long gown gently gathered at the shoulders, with a batwing-sleeve effect created through a complicated system of lacing and oblique drawstrings along the arm. The sensuality of the silken pleats enhanced by the classic, timeless simplicity of the cut produced a modern garment freeing the female body from artificial constraint.

Fortuny also drew on the finest Renaissance Italian velvets for his own print designs, creating a wide range of patterns to match the individual style of each garment, often applying the print to the fabric only after it had been cut, and sometimes not until it had been sewn.

Group photograph of the Bevilacqua staff. This firm, founded by Luigi Bevilacqua, manufactures silks and trim, and has practiced traditional Venetian weaving techniques for over 120 years.

Mariano Fortuny, silk velvet print. Early twentieth century. This pattern is freely drawn from those of sixteenth-century Italian velvets.

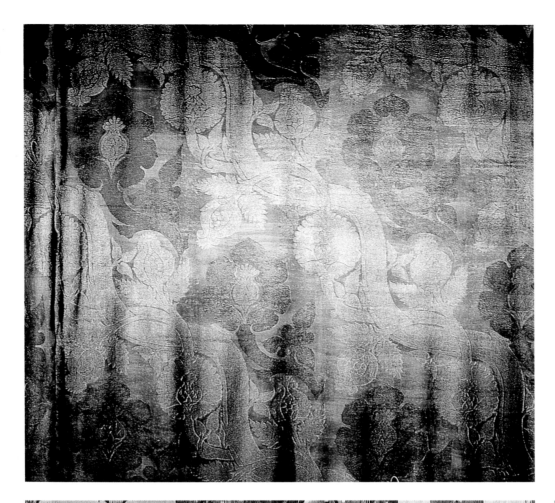

Mariano Fortuny's fabric collection in his Rome studio-museum.
Photographic archives, Museo Fortuny, Venice.

Textile design gained in importance during the twentieth century, finally emerging as an art form in its own right. Naturalistic forms were first stylized, and then became totally abstract. Patterns designed in terms of function (the style of the final garment) were often printed rather than woven, which facilitated faithful reproduction of the artist's original work.

The growing preference for printed silks developed logically from the simplification of feminine fashion, and the need to meet the demands of mass production and lower manufacturing costs.

The theories developed by English artists Christopher Dresser and William Morris in the second half of the nineteenth century contributed substantially to freeing textile design from the historical nostalgia that was still prevalent at the beginning of the twentieth century. A successful textile pattern must be designed in terms of the specific material on which it will be printed and the material's ultimate use. Textile patterns are also repeated, a factor differentiating them from similar patterns used in painting. William Morris's most important contribution to the genre was to reject naturalistic three-dimensional patterns in favor of a two-dimensional decorative repertory applied to printed fabrics and to patterned silks woven on mechanical Jacquard looms.

At the turn of the twentieth century, French designers such as Eugène Grasset wrote studies on the ornamental use of plant motifs, confirming a predilection in textile design for the naturalistic. At the same time, however, they explored methods for creating more stylized designs. For example, Grasset divided fabric into rectangular sections which he combined with sinuous curves, the former representing the geometry of the organic world, the latter its vitality. The motifs for patterned silks presented at the *Exposition de la soie* organized by the Musée Galliera in 1906 (now the Musée de la Mode et du Costume), exemplified this new style of organic representation, which also reflected the free-flowing aesthetic of the Art Nouveau movement.

Belgian architect and interior decorator Henry van de Velde viewed textile design as a constituent part of life, which itself was considered as an artistic whole. He was fascinated by artistic form for its own sake, and pioneered the use of abstract shapes. In 1900, he was given an opportunity to put his theories to practice when he received a number of commissions from the Krefeld silk weavers.

Roses, by Paul Follot. Lampas silk woven in 1911 by Tassinari et Chatel. This design of stylized roses by sculptor and interior decorator Paul Follot was later to become famous.

The work of the Wiener Werkstätte group set textile design firmly on the path of abstraction. The Vienna-based group, founded in 1903 by architect Josef Hoffmann, painter Koloman Moser, and businessman Fritz Waerndorfer, was originally conceived as a cooperative for the production of hand-crafted artifacts. The increasing importance of textiles in virtually every aspect of the group's design projects led, in 1910, to the creation of a department devoted entirely to fabrics and fashion, and in 1916 to the inauguration of a specialized retail outlet. Wiener Werkstätte designs featured unusual color combinations and were printed on a range of fabrics including silk, cotton, and linen. They exemplified contemporary taste for simplified abstract and geometric forms used in conjunction with stylized figurative patterns. The Wiener Werkstätte adventure came to an end in 1932.

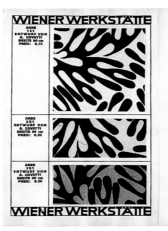

Catalogue of silk samples. c. 1912. Wiener Werkstätte.

Arabesque, by Anny Schröder. c. 1920. Fabric and lounging pajamas. Wiener Werkstätte.

Unlike the Wiener Werkstätte, which marketed its products commercially, the Bauhaus, founded by Walter Gropius in 1919 at Weimar and moved in 1924 to Dessau, was intended to serve solely as a school and a laboratory for new ideas. Encouraged by Gropius, whose aim was to raise handicrafts to the status of painting and sculpture, the group opened various workshops, including a weaving workshop which remained in operation throughout the life of the Bauhaus movement. This workshop's student weavers developed the concept of textile patterns based on the structure and texture of the fabric itself.

The experiments of the Wiener Werkstätte and the Bauhaus facilitated the introduction of abstract patterns into textile design, raising its status by turning it into a medium for purely artistic creation. A perfect illustration of the new approach can be seen in the works of Raoul Dufy and Sonia Delaunay.

Fruit of the Hesperides, by
Dagobert Peche. 1919. Fabric
and lounging pajamas.
Wiener Werkstätte.

worked with a sea theme which in 1925 inspired the famous silver-brocaded satin entitled *Sea Horses, Whales, and Sea Shells*; and the pattern for *Amphitrites*, a laminette silk brocade used by Paul Poiret for a cape.

Textile design also became an important element in Sonia Delaunay's work. In 1923, she created patterns for a Lyon silk weaver, and opened her own studio in Paris. There she designed hand-printed silk scarfs that were genuine works of art, combining carefully organized forms with lively variations in color. This foray into clothing textile design gave her an opportunity to develop her pictorial language in three dimensions, a new departure from the restrictive two dimensions of traditional painting. Delaunay consistently viewed pattern in terms of ultimate function, and paid meticulous attention to simplicity and clarity of form, choice of color, and the way in which her patterns would move when worn. She worked primarily with silk prints, thus adding value to the material—as did Raoul Dufy—for both manufacturers and couturiers.

Sonia Delaunay, *Simultaneous, No. 204.* 1927. Print crepe de chine by Bianchini-Férier. Musée des Arts de la Mode et du Textile (collection UCAD), Paris. Delaunay designed her "simultaneous" fabrics using geometric motifs in bright colors adapted to the cut of the final garment.

Design studio for Lyon silk at

La Viabert mill, Villeurbanne.

c. 1930. Roger-Viollet, Paris.

The artistic renewal focused on silk did not escape the notice of fabric merchant François Ducharne, who in 1920 opened the doors of his newly created firm in Paris, appointing Michel Dubost at the head of its design studio. Dubost was a silk designer who in 1918 had been named instructor of the floral-design course at the Lyon school of fine arts. In this capacity he accompanied his students on annual trips to Paris and, through the president of the French silk trade association, M. Fructus, had their work published in *La Soierie de Lyon*, a silk-industry trade journal. Dubost specialized in luxury patterned silks, and in 1912 he designed *Alhambra*, a lampas silk with a pattern of birds behind a series of Hispano-Mauresque arcades. This was followed in 1922 by his *Blue-bird*, a famous brocatelle woven at the Lyon silk-weaving school. At the 1925 Paris Exposition Internationale des Arts Décoratifs (from which the term "Art Deco" is derived), he presented *Bird in Light*, a gold lamé romaine crepe woven in a pattern based on research carried out by his scientist friend Edouard Monod-Herzen on form and movement in nature, a subject in vogue at the time.

Lampas silk after a design by

Suzanne Lalique, woven

between 1920 and 1926.

Reproduced in 1934 by Prelle

for the transatlantic ocean

liner *Le Paris*.

Dubost's design studio was located on the rue Tourlaque in Montmartre. It employed some thirty designers with close connections to Parisian artistic circles, including Bernard Lorjou, Yvonne Mottet, Guy de Chaunac (subsequently famous for his tapestries), Reverend Father Dom Robert, painter Jean Peltier, and Suzanne Janin—who was hired on the basis of a recommendation from Monod-Herzen.

Ducharne was a firm believer in the value of originality and, in order to afford maximum creative freedom to his designers, he reserved a large portion of his production for prints. He also understood the contemporary trend towards simpler, shorter dresses, and the desire of newly active women for practical clothing, a shift which forced silk manufacturers to modernize their product. Heavily patterned weaves began to disappear in favor of fluid plain-weave silks that focused attention on the basic cut of the garment. Printed rather than woven patterns thus became the natural alternative to solid colors.

As the head of Ducharne's design studio, Michel Dubost devoted considerable effort to encouraging his young colleagues and helping them develop their own artistic vision and color sense. Unhappily, this ideal training-ground for young talent was forced to close its doors in 1931 as a result of the 1929 stock-market crash. Bernard Lorjou and Yvonne Mottet moved to Staron silk makers, which had only recently begun operations. Jean Peltier and Suzanne Janin opened their own design studio and continued to work for Ducharne, who manufactured fabric until the early 1960s. Suzanne Janin's witty, poetic prints were often used by designer Elsa Schiaparelli, to whose whimsical sense of creativity they were ideally suited.

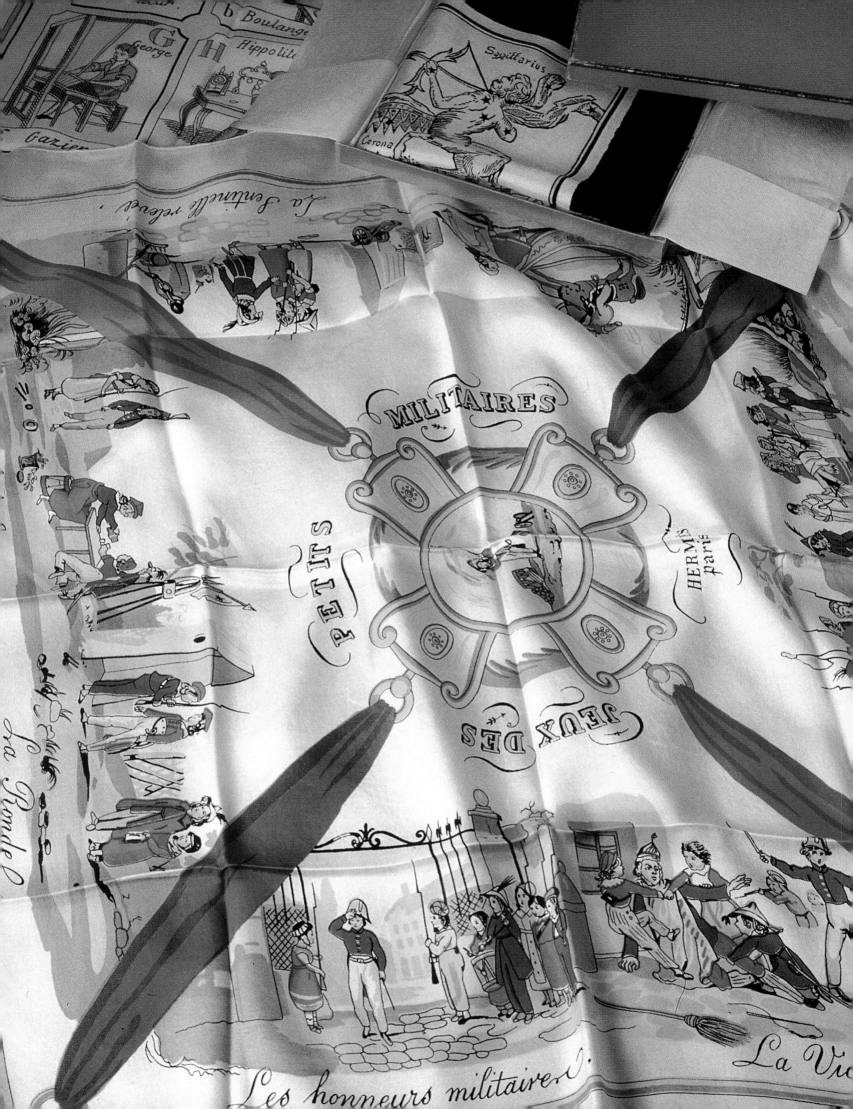

Jeux des petits militaires
(Young Soldiers at Play).
1946. One of the first silk
scarfs by Hermès.
Hermès archives, Paris.

Sample book of silk prints for
neckties by Ratti.
Ratti archives, Como.

Silk Scales New Heights with Haute Couture

The beauty of silk, its texture, and the unique way in which it reflects light make it the ideal material for *haute couture* and original design. Eminent couturiers find in silk the ideal medium for the expression of their individual styles. Some design straight from the fabric, as a challenge to their inventiveness; some sketch the design first and then procure the type of silk best suited to its realization; while others combine the two methods. *Haute couture* has traditionally served as a hothouse of new ideas, an impetus for fabric innovation, and the perfect arena for testing new techniques capable of exploiting the properties of fabric to the utmost.

Although silk first entered the realm of daytime women's apparel through the semi-formal day dress, it is with the cocktail dress—which treads a fine line between daring and simplicity—and the evening dress that this material can be seen at its most opulent. In the past, pure silk was the habitual clothing fabric for an entire class of the well-to-do and wealthy. Today the invention of synthetic and artificial yarns, and the development of blends, have made silk a rare and precious commodity. How-

ever, thanks to the work of a few couturiers and fashion designers dedicated to expanding its possibilities, it has scaled new heights in the twentieth century.

In the 1930s, Madeleine Vionnet, a trained seamstress who designed her models by draping fabric over tiny articulated wooden mannequins, invented an entirely new way of dealing with fabric and exploiting its fluidity: the bias-cut. The importance of this innovation was underscored by Guillaume Garnier, who wrote in the catalogue of the exhibition *Paris, Couture, années 1930:* "Whereas the twenties saw the reign of the straight unfitted little dress that concealed the curve of the body, the thirties pioneered the expression of anatomically exact formal perception and the exaltation of movement. The bias-cut obeys the laws of this revolutionary aesthetic to the letter, revealing the figure without constraining it, using drapery and

Dress by Patou, jewelry by Jean Fouquet, shoes by Hellstern. 1927.

floating panels to accompany, emphasize, and highlight every gesture." The styles of this period lengthened and streamlined the feminine silhouette, accenting the natural curves of the body with clothing that is fitted yet affords freedom of movement. The neoclassical idiom evident in various artistic fields at the time also fostered the emergence of a purist clothing style inspired by Antiquity. Madeleine Vionnet was an early adept of the cult that venerated classical Greece and Rome, and based her own work on the aesthetic principles evident in antique statuary: clothing that flows over the body naturally, covering it completely while also allowing freedom of movement. It was in this spirit that Vionnet invented her new geometry of fabric. The bias-cut allowed pleats to fall with a natural drape, and skirts often had flying panels attached to them. Floating drapery was loosely attached at a few key points on the garment. Vionnet also achieved visual harmony by eliminating complicated accessories and restricting her color range. She exploited the fabric's intrinsic properties, such as transparency or the contrast between top- and under-side. By using cloth in extra-large widths, she minimized the need for seams. Her fluid, draped styles required lightweight fabrics that would hang well, and she worked closely with Lyon silk maker Bianchini-Férier, who was celebrated in the 1930s for a range of silk crepes including romaine, crepe marocain, and georgette. For Vionnet, Bianchini-Férier developed *rosalba* crepe, a blend of silk and artificial yarns. At the same time, Ducharne was designing fabric patterns to enhance the cut of individual garments, as for a 1924 evening dress in black romaine crepe with a brocaded flame motif. The Vionnet couture house, which closed in 1939, was also responsible for the development of hand-cut silk velvet, a totally new technique.

Another luminary of the period was Madame Grès. Born Germaine Krebs, she changed her name to Alice Barton when she began her career as a seamstress with the Alix couture house in 1934, and changed it once again when she opened her own business in the very early 1940s. Madame Grès also drew her inspiration from Greek statuary, modeling her fabrics by hand like a sculptor. Her command of drapery was consummate, as can be seen in models with hand-tucked and sewn bodices that control the fall of the loose tubular pleated skirts below. For this type of dress, Madame Grès used silk and artificial-silk jersey woven in extra-large widths.

Meanwhile, during the Roaring Twenties, Jean Patou and Gabrielle Chanel provided their own novel responses to the modern woman's desire for freedom and indepen-

Right:

Madeleine Grès, silk/jersey evening dress. Spring 1952. Musée de la Mode et du Costume, Paris.

dence. The new, postwar woman was active and athletic. For her, Chanel designed clothes in tweed and silk jersey that could be worn all day long. Patou launched a similar style, inaugurating the "twin set," a pullover sweater with matching cardigan to be worn with coordinated skirts and accessories in silk or wool. This new style galvanized the knitting industry and created new ways to use silk for luxury clothing.

Elsa Schiaparelli was also famed for her sweaters, which she presented first on the rue de l'Université, and then at 4 rue de la Paix. In 1935, she moved to the Place Vendôme. Schiaparelli favored recently developed fabrics, especially artificial ones, because of their lower cost and innovative properties. She worked closely with the Colcombet weaving mill on the development of rayons with unusual visual and tactile properties. In 1932, she designed an entire collection in rayon crepe, and introduced two artificial jerseys: *jersala,* similar to satin; and *jersarelli,* a lustrous crepe with a matte reverse side. In 1934, she introduced rayon tulle. Schiaparelli also took especial delight in using fabrics for unaccustomed purposes, such as silk taffeta or shantung for raincoats. She had a predilection for silk prints, which gave her a large field in which to exercise a lively imagination often inspired by surrealist painting.

The *Carrier Swallow* design was created in 1939 by Suzanne Janin-Peltier for Ducharne. Elsa Schiaparelli was particularly fond of this design, and chose it for the dress she wore to a dinner held at the Eiffel Tower on 29 June 1939.

Right:
Elsa Schiaparelli, three evening dresses with bustles. 1939. Photograph by François Kollar. The pattern on the dress shown in the center is *Woman with Poodle* designed by painter Jean Peltier for Ducharne.

As François Ducharne was to write in the catalogue for the exhibition *Les folles années de la soie:* "I worked closely with her, submitting original ideas that she adopted and adapted for her own purposes." Between 1938 and 1940, Suzanne Janin's designs for Ducharne were often used by Elsa Schiaparelli on silk crepe and crepon. These patterns include Christmas crackers, jam pots, tiny wooden shoes, and a stylized bird carrying a billet-doux in its beak. The latter was a particularly successful motif that—symbolically, perhaps—Elsa Schiaparelli was to adopt as her own for a print silk dress she wore to a dinner at the Eiffel Tower on 29 June 1939. That same year she added bustles to her formal models, and for one of them used a silk designed by Jean Peltier, *Woman with Poodle*, a glance backward at the late nineteenth-century woman wittily underscored by the cut of the dress and pattern of the fabric.

Christian Dior started out in 1938 as a modeler for Robert Piguet, moving in 1941 to become a designer at Lucien Lelong. He opened his own couture house in 1946 at 30 avenue Montaigne. Dior's method was to sketch the main lines for his models on paper, and then have his technical assistant Marguerite Carré make up muslin prototypes in her workrooms. He would then select the most successful and indicate the fabrics to be used for the finished garments. When the final models were completed, he added further detailing before presenting them to the public. Dior made lavish use of silk for his collections and worked closely with all the major silk makers, gradually turning to heavier silks as his style evolved from 1947 to 1957 towards a more streamlined silhouette.

Dior presented his first collection on 12 January 1947. Immediately dubbed the "New Look" by Carmel Snow, editor-in-chief of the fashion magazine *Harper's Bazaar*, this collection marked the birth of a style that has since become a classic. The bustline was high, the shoulders natural and rounded, the waistline fitted. Long, full skirts falling to well below the knee were worn over petticoats and crinolines. Dior's succeeding collections confirmed this original vision of a rhythmic, graceful, extremely feminine silhouette. The major fabric used was silk—in chiffon, organza, faille, satin, and shantung. Although the Spring 1950 collection was more subdued, the lines remained swaying and rhythmic, and the wearer enveloped in gossamer silks: chiffons, georgettes, organzas; and lightweight plain, finely pleated, or artfully draped taffetas. Dior designed fairy-tale evening dresses, a prime example being his famous floor-length

Christian Dior, evening coat in navy silk sateen worn over a velvet dress. 1949. Photograph by Maywald. The drape of the heavy silk sateen coat underscores the femininity of a full-skirted silhouette fitted at the waist.

"Mexique" gown in brown silk tulle embroidered with gold crescent moons which was included in his Autumn/Winter 1951/1952 collection. It was at this point that Dior's style became more streamlined, the cuts less complicated, the bustline longer. These were the H-, Y-, and A-line styles shown in Dior's collections for Autumn/Winter 1952/1953, Autumn/Winter 1954/1955, Spring/Summer 1955, and Autumn/Winter 1955/1956. This new cut required stiffer fabrics: faille, velvet, taffeta, heavy ottoman, and blends of wool and silk. Tulle and satin continued to be used for evening dresses, with the addition of brocades. Dior often used print fabrics designed exclusively for him. Many of these were floral, but some featured more original motifs based on such diverse sources of inspiration as the shimmer of butterfly wings, prehistoric paintings, and oriental carpets. Christian Dior also supported the revival of complicated silk-weaving techniques such as *velours sabres* and warp prints, specialized fabrics which he used mainly for evening dresses.

Whereas Dior sketched his models on paper before then having them made up in muslin, Cristóbal Balenciaga worked directly with the fabric. Balenciaga began his career as a tailor's assistant in Madrid, and in 1910 opened his own workshop in San Sebastián. It was there he founded his first couture house in 1915, following it with a second one in Madrid. He moved to Barcelona in 1935, but was soon forced by the Spanish Civil War to move again. This time he went to Paris, where in 1937 he opened his establishment at 10 avenue George V, and soon presented his first collection. He retired in 1968.

Balenciaga worked like an architect or a sculptor, placing his major emphasis on the cut of the garment, always seeking new ways to organize the line of his models. Waistlines disappeared for his famous tunic and shirt dresses of 1955 and 1957; were emphasized by exaggerated curves at the hip; or raised, as for his 1959 empire styles. He was particularly interested in sleeves and designed numerous variations for them, by far the most famous of which was the "melon" sleeve of 1950. He transformed the overall silhouette by exaggerating the shoulders, lowering necklines, and pushing hiplines out at the back. Balenciaga's unequalled mastery of form gave increased prominence to his fabrics, which had to be carefully selected for the cut to attain the desired perfection. Everyone who knew Balenciaga and his work recognized his fascination with fabric, of which he was the ultimate connoisseur.

Like other great couturiers before him, Balenciaga worked closely with all the great silk makers, forming unofficial partnerships with some of them, such as a Swiss firm headed by Abraham and Gustave Zumsteg (co-founder with Ludwig Abraham). During the 1950s, Gustave Zumsteg attempted to produce a silk fabric with the texture of cotton gauze. The result was "gazar," a silk woven from slightly irregular matte slubbed yarn affording a magnificent rustic effect. Gazar is a lightweight fabric that hangs well and can be artfully molded, and Balenciaga was an acknowledged master

Cocktail ensemble by Cristóbal Balenciaga. 1962. Red silk taffeta warp-print with black polka dots. Musée de la Mode et du Costume, Paris.
The cut of the vivid taffeta gives this model the dynamic movement of a flamenco dancer.

Olivier Lapidus, coat in brown sand silk by Bucol worn over brown plaid wool/silk trousers and a silk chiffon sweater knit by Buche. From the *Hymne à la soie* collection. Autumn/Winter 1994/1995.

at exploiting its sculptural properties, with successes such as the short black cocktail dress from the Autumn/Winter 1967/1968 collection, a sheath flaring at the bustline into four points held by rhinestone straps, and the black "cream-puff" cape worn like an intricately sculptured ruff over a black crepe sheath. Abraham and Zumsteg wove gazar in various weights known respectively as *shatuna, zagar,* and *supergazar,* all of which were used by Balenciaga. The Spanish couturier also liked to experiment with materials such as laminates based on spun viscose and the lizard satin made by the firm of Bucol, using them for the waterproof raincoats featured in most of his collections through 1968. Balenciaga used synthetics alone, or blended with silk. In 1964, the firm of Hurel supplied him with a patterned silk/acetate velvet, and Chatillon-Mouly-Roussel with a patterned cellophane and silk blend. He particularly appreciated fabrics of high technical complexity, such as a silk tulle embroidered with a synthetic stiffener, a lacy silk tulle embroidered with braid by Marescot, and of course warp prints and *velours sabres.*

French couturiers forged strong links with silk weavers, as exemplified by Olivier Lapidus's Autumn/Winter 1994/1995 collection entitled *L'Hymne à la soie.* This collection was designed to strengthen existing bonds between couturiers, silk weavers, and all the satellite crafts connected with both. The goal was to reconcile traditional craftsmanship and mass production, and to demonstrate as never before that one of *haute couture*'s primary missions is to serve as a crucible for the experiments and contacts that can lead, in the words of Olivier Lapidus himself, "to a humanistic working partnership." This collection was a showcase for the technical prowess of all major contemporary French silk weavers. It included a coat in imitation silk fur by Bucol, a dress in frayed silk chiffon with silk velvet ribbons produced jointly by weavers Hurel and Julien Faure, and an evening dress in Nattier-blue silk and eighteen-carat gold brocade woven by Brochier with a bodice in hand-cut satin by Bucol. Here was living proof that, even when this degree of technical superiority is required, the mechanical Jacquard loom is indeed capable of producing artfully woven fabrics in large widths. With his Spring/Summer 1995 collection entitled *Jeux*

Crushed silk chiffon shirt by Issey Miyake. Spring/Summer 1995.

d'optique, Olivier Lapidus confirmed the capacity of French *haute couture* to stimulate innovative developments in contemporary fabric. In this instance, he sought to create optical effects by approaching silk in new ways, and drew on the principle of the hologram to design patterns which give an unprecedented illusion of depth.

Other designers have also left an indelible mark on the history of silk and of fashion. The celebrated Japanese couturier Issey Miyake brings an original vision to clothing, designing voluminous and dynamic styles that highlight the movement of the body in space. From the presentation of his first collection in New York in 1971, he has carried out extensive textile research. Silk featured prominently in his collections during the late seventies and early eighties, following which Miyake then began to concentrate on the improved potential for permanent pleating and crushing offered by artificial and synthetic fabrics, especially polyester. His experiments were successful, and in 1988 he re-applied the principle of permanent pleating to silk, designing a series of crushed silk-chiffon shirts for his Spring/Summer 1995 collection.

Marc Audibet, impelled by a desire to offer contemporary clothing in resolutely contemporary fabrics, sought from 1982 onwards to design woven stretch silks that would follow the natural contours of the body, truly "dressing" it without diminishing freedom of movement. He also pioneered stretch silk taffeta for his collections of 1984 and 1985. Other designers, such as Mariot Chanet, have made use of woven silk blended with around ten percent Lycra. They appreciate the intrinsic properties of this stretch silk, which is more flexible and—because of the Lycra's capacity to expand and retract—becomes more or less transparent or opaque depending on the wearer's movements.

The 1990s witnessed a renewal of interest in silk. Factors contributing to this trend include an interest in oriental styles, general recognition of the achievement of oriental designers, the rapid development of washed silk, and a more openly expressed appreciation of true luxury.

Olivier Lapidus, floor-length Nattier blue silk dress with 18-carat gold brocade. Brocade and hand-cut satin bodice by Bucol. From the *Hymne à la soie* collection. Autumn/Winter 1994/1995.

The
Silk
Revival

During the nineteenth century, the silkworms of France's once-thriving breeding industry were virtually annihilated by an epidemic of pebrine, a disease particular to the *Bombyx mori*. However, thanks in large part to experiments carried out in the Cévennes—a mountainous area to the south-east of the Massif Central—and its neighboring regions, silkworms are once again being bred successfully in France. In addition, original hand-powered Jacquard looms still owned by a few weavers in Lyon, Tours, and Nîmes, are being used to reproduce the antique silks that constitute such an important part of the French and European artistic heritage. Saint-Étienne and the surrounding region maintain their traditions of fine silk trim- and ribbon-making, and Parisian *haute couture* houses provide an important outlet for both figured and printed silks.

The demand for reproductions of antique silks comes primarily from the furnishing market, which provides the necessary financial investment no longer assured by royal patronage. Although modern automated Jacquard looms have significantly reduced the cost of producing figured silks such as damasks, brocades, and lamés, modern design has tended to focus on printed patterns woven on plain or box looms.

France's "silk country" covers several regions. Silkworm breeders and filament reelers are concentrated in the Cévennes and Gard; throwers in the Ardèche and Drôme; trim- and ribbon-makers in the Loire and Haute-Loire; industrial weavers in Lyon, and cottage weavers in Isère. Dyers and finishers are dispersed throughout all these regions. Despite expansion beyond fixed regional borders, each craft maintains its individual identity.

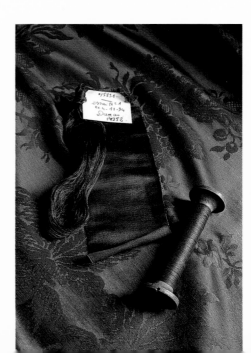

Test-dyeing prior to re-weaving the fabric. The skeins of dyed silk serve as a guide for reproduction of the fabric. Georges Le Manach archives, Tours.

THE REBIRTH OF SERICULTURE

Evidence of a deeply rooted sericulture tradition in the Cévennes, Gard, Ardèche, and Drôme regions in southern France can be seen today in the distinctive architecture of surviving silkworm breeding houses. These buildings are on several floors, each dedicated to one of the five separate phases in the development of the tiny larvae, from seed to cocoon. In olden times the mulberry was known as the "golden tree." Today, the area where it once grew is traversed by the new "silk road," narrow country lanes twisting through a magnificent landscape dotted with local museums housed in former silkworm breeding houses and silk-throwing mills.

The Cévennes

In the year 1853, just before the disastrous pebrine onslaught, the Cévennes region of France produced twenty-six thousand metric tons of cocoons. The last silk-reeling factory in Saint-Jean-de-Gard did not close its doors until 1964. In 1972, the pupils of the Monoblet elementary school, encouraged by their principal Michel Costa, embarked on an experiment in silkworm breeding that gradually attracted the interest of adults in the community, many of them former silkworm breeders who had been forced by declining profits to abandon their profession. This group eventually decided to plant orchards around their town with an experimental species of Japanese mulberry tree. Their initiative led, in 1977, to the formation of Sérica, an association for the development of sericulture in the Cévennes. By 1986, the association boasted a membership of two hundred silk breeders, and native Cévennes silk is now reeled, woven, and marketed in a wide range of finished products. In Saint-Hippolyte-du-Fort there is even a company that manufactures silk apparel.

A laboratory for *in vitro* duplication of the experimental mulberry tree is housed in a cottage in Puechlong, deep in the Cévennes countryside. This laboratory also has an orchard of small Japanese mulberry trees, known as *Kokusos 21*. Today over fifty thousand mulberry trees have been replanted in the Cévennes region alone and, thanks to these local initiatives, Sérica has been invited to take part in the Eurochrysalide project, a cooperative effort sponsored by major French and

international laboratories working on advanced silk technology. Eurochrysalide is also sponsoring a plan to build an experimental silkworm breeding station in the Ardèche. With the revival of sericulture in France and other European countries such as Italy, Spain, and Portugal, the silk weavers of Lyon are hoping to achieve a twenty-five percent reduction in silk imports from China, which at the moment enjoys a virtual monopoly on the market. China has an annual silk production totalling 32,000 metric tons which accounts for ninety percent of raw silk production worldwide. France, on the other hand, has an annual production of only six hundred tons.

A team of geneticists at the French national institute for agronomical research (INRA) is working on the development of a new hybrid silkworm species that will be disease-resistant and spin a higher-quality filament than Chinese silkworms. INRA is also experimenting with new breeding techniques based on the use of artificial nutrients—a radical departure from the traditional image of sericulture illustrated in ancient Chinese watercolors. Research is also being conducted into possible medical and pharmaceutical applications for sericin, an amino acid extracted from the silkworm cocoon. The Japanese, meanwhile, are attempting to double the length of the silk filament out of which each cocoon is spun.

The Musée de la Soie at Saint-Hippolyte-du-Fort houses outstanding silks donated by Sérica and independent local weavers, and a comprehensive exhibition on the life cycle of the silkworm. The Musée Cévenol (museum of the Cevennes) at Saint-Jean-du-Gard also has a large sericulture exhibit. Next to the museum stands the Maison Rouge, one of the largest of the old silk-reeling factories, which was built in 1856 and remained in operation until 1964. In May 1994 the two towns organized the first Cévennes silk festival. Le Vigan also has a Musée Cévenol, housed in a converted eighteenth-century reeling factory located in the old medieval quarter of the town on the banks of the Arre River. In 1850, twenty-five thousand acres of mulberry trees were planted in the Le Vigan area alone. The museum, most of which is devoted to exhibits connected with silk, has in its collection an eighteenth-century loom for weaving silk stockings and a collection of embroidered stockings from the same era. Several period dresses *à la française* made from silk taffeta woven in Lyon, Nîmes, and Avignon are also on display.

Ardèche

This region to the east of the Cévennes was once a silk-throwing center, and some of the old throwing mills with their characteristic vaulted workrooms still stand along the banks of local rivers. Numerous efforts to preserve this precious heritage have been undertaken, encouraged by the creation, in 1991, of a departmental conservation commission for the museums of the Ardèche.

The Pont-de-Bridon throwing mill at Vals-les-Bains, built over 150 years ago, is still in operation. The mill is now fitted with the most advanced modern equipment, which has improved quality and increased output of the yarn processed for use in silk veils, lace, crepe, embroideries, and so on.

At Villeneuve-de-Berg stands Le Pradel, the estate once owned by the distinguished Renaissance agronomist Olivier de Serres, who played a key role in the development of sericulture under Henri IV.

Sericulture has been practiced in the Ardèche region since the seventeenth century. In addition to the large fairs held in Aubenas, Privas, Joyeuse, Lablachère, Largentière, and Tournon, markets in all the small villages where silk was woven also served as outlets for silkworm cocoons and thrown silk yarn. In order to meet the demand for raw silk from weavers in Lyon and Saint-Étienne, vast numbers of mulberry trees were planted in the region at the beginning of the nineteenth century. By 1846, the number of trees had increased to over eight million, but a mere ten years later French sericulture was on its knees, destroyed by the pebrine epidemic that decimated generations of silkworms. Louis Pasteur was called in to find both the cause of the disease and its cure. When, after five years of intensive research, he finally succeeded, it was already too late. French sericulture had declined irreparably, and the only way the Ardèche throwing mills could continue to make a profit was by processing raw silk yarn imported from Japan, and later China.

In 1973, the French national association for the production and promotion of silk attempted in vain to relaunch sericulture in France. It was not until some years later, when the original 1972 Cévennes experiments began to bear fruit, that a few silkworm breeders cautiously re-entered the field. Steady progress culminated in 1986 with the creation of the Vivarais sericulture commission at Aubenas, the nineteenth-century capital of the silk-throwing craft.

Drôme

A former silkworm-breeding farm at Saillans in the Drôme region, in south-east France, has been converted into a modern sericulture research center. Displays at the center on view to the public include an exhibit explaining the life cycle of the silkworm from seed to cocoon. Vivid reproductions of ancient Chinese watercolors also on show at the center provide visible evidence that basic silk production techniques have changed little over the centuries.

The modern silkworm breeding center at Aubres, near Nyons, presents a slightly different picture, since here the breeding cycle is arrested before completion in order to extract silk proteins for use in cosmetics. Exhibits in the silk museum at Montboucher-sur-Jabron, near Montélimar, display all the phases in silkworm development from hatching to cocoon spinning, as well as the techniques of silk reeling and throwing.

In his guide to silk in the Rhône-Alpes region, Dominique Voisin describes a curious local custom practiced in the past: "Here, silkworm eggs were called 'children' and incubated inside small bags worn by peasant women under their skirts. When the eggs were ready to hatch, the woman would extract a hairpin from her chignon, pierce the eggs with it, and place the newborn 'children' in baskets woven by the head of the household." In other regions silkworm eggs were incubated in bags worn by peasant women between their breasts.

Hybrid silkworm cocoons (foreground) shown with cocoons spun by the two parent species.

CONTEMPORARY FURNISHING FABRICS

Lyon

The main street in Lyon's Croix-Rousse district is still lined today with the workrooms where the city's *canuts* lived and labored. The architecture of these buildings makes them easy to identify, since they were built to accommodate a fifteen-foot high Jacquard loom in the main room, with space enough above the loom to provide access to the overhead mechanism in which pattern cards were inserted. Today, however, these houses have fallen silent: the clatter of the old looms and the protest songs sung by the weavers no longer resound between their walls. Many silk weavers went bankrupt during the economic depression of the 1930s, and World War II accelerated the decline of the industry still further. Only the hardiest firms survived, some of them joining forces in order to control the entire production cycle more efficiently.

Although a few designers still work independently, as in the eighteenth century, most Lyon silk weavers maintain in-house design departments for creation of their annual collections. They purchase their yarn from importers and have it dyed, woven, and finished by the region's network of subcontractors.

Lyon's colorful past has not, however, been forgotten. Although many antique looms were broken up and used as firewood during the war, making them extremely rare today, at the Maison des Canuts retired weavers still operate looms built in Jacquard's time, and a hand-operated draw-loom with interchangeable drawstrings is also on display.

Nearby stands the municipal trim factory, purchased by the city when its owner Henriette Letourneau reached the age of seventy and decided to retire. The building was saved from the wrecker's ball by an association named *Soierie Vivante* (Living Silk) dedicated to the preservation and promotion of Lyon's rich textile heritage.

The Musée Historique des Tissus features displays of most of the antique fabrics woven in both East and West described in the present work. The museum's exhibits form a comprehensive survey of the history of silk, covering every period and every style.

Despite the many crises that have afflicted the city's silk industry over the centuries, Lyon remains the undisputed capital of contemporary silk design, and a wellspring of traditional craftsmanship that can still be drawn on today for the reproduction of antique fabrics. Lyon furnishing fabrics are still of outstanding quality, and are characterized by their sumptuous patterns woven in complex combinations of yarn (gold on silk, silver on silk, and silk on silk chenille), the richness and diversity of their colors, and their artful combination of contrasting textures (taffeta and satin, velvet and taffeta, and so on).

Isère

This region south-east of Lyon has, over the centuries, been home to every craft connected with silk, from throwing to weaving. The firm of Schwarzenbach, for example, is housed in a throwing mill founded over 150 years ago at La Tour-du-Pin. Schwarzenbach is famed for its thrown and gimped (creped, crushed, crimped, bouclé, shirred) silk yarns. The company has recently added modern variations to its primary range of products, such as yarns incorporating stainless steel, nickel, glass, and polyamide resins, which it sells to industry and avant-garde fashion designers.

Guipure, or covered yarn, is highly important for the production and historic reproduction of brocades and damasks. For gold brocades, the guilder concocts his "gold liqueur" according to the intensity and nuance of the shade he wishes to obtain. Hand-crafted gold-encased thread was one of the great specialties of fifteenth-century Florence: modern imitations are made by using galvanoplasty to guild a core made of copper.

The major specialty of the Isère region, and one highly prized by today's Lyon silk weavers, is printed silk. Silk was once printed from engraved copper plates, but today advanced laser technology is used. The center of this economic and artistic activity is located in Bourgoin-Jallieu and the surrounding area. The Musée Victor-Charreton features displays devoted to the secrets of printing *à la Lyonnaise*. A new museum designed by architect Pierre Schall and scheduled for completion in 1996 will house an extensive display of all silk printing techniques, from the engraved copper plate of the past to the laser beam of today. Several Bourgoin-Jallieu firms specialize in producing frames for silk screen printing. One of the most prominent firms in the area is Marcel Gandit, which over the past forty-five years has been executing photogravure designs for Hermès scarfs and now has more than nine hundred patterns to its credit. Some of these patterns require as many as forty separate frames, one for each color in the design. The members of Gandit's design department, who account for two-thirds of the firm's total work force, must often meet specifications that allow for a margin of error measured in a fraction of a thousandth of an inch. The international renown of the firm is due largely to the talents of these skilled designers. They are given full responsibility for a particular design, and are encouraged to express their own artistic vision and style—their "signature." As M. Gandit explains, "Our goal is to match the right designer to the right design. This requires a profound understanding of the artistic temperament that will produce the best result."

Bourgoin-Jallieu is also home to dyers, finishers, and other printing firms specializing in silk. One of the most outstanding of these is Memoz. The Memoz workshops contain impressive printing tables measuring over three hundred feet long. Freshly printed lengths of fabric are hung up to dry above them like giant canopies, and create an exotic and constantly changing décor. Memoz was chosen to reproduce the warp-dyed velvet for Napoleon's bedchamber at Fontainebleau. Because of the recessed texture of the warp, used solely for the velvet nap and its pattern, sixty-five separate screens were required for dyeing one thousand yards of warp yarn, which was then used by Tassinari et Chatel for weaving just one hundred yards of finished velvet.

The Saint-Étienne Region

As described in a previous chapter, during the period immediately preceding the 1831 *canuts'* revolt many employers sought less expensive sources of labor in the Bas-Dauphiné region and the area north of the Loire river. Although their quest was largely unsuccessful, a silk-weaving tradition took root in these areas which never completely died out. In 1950, the commune of La Bâtie-Mongascon still boasted over fifty small workshops and eighteen silk manufacturers. A minor tradition, perhaps, but one commemorated in Saint-Étienne by the Maison du Tisserand, built in the same style as the weavers' houses found in Lyon's Croix-Rousse district. The craft of weaving silk ribbon has an especially long history in Saint-Étienne, where it reached its apogee at the end of the seventeenth century. Today

Skeins of raw silk, which are soaked in warm oily soapsuds prior to dyeing in order to soften the natural gum they contain.

Gold thread used in trim produced by Carlhian. Skeins of silk are packaged in groups of twenty-five before being baled for shipment.

Damask being woven on a mechanical loom. Prelle archives, Lyon.

Hermès, *Texas Flora and Fauna.* Spring/Summer 1987 collection. Hermès archives, Paris.

Hand printing Hermès scarfs. Hermès archives, Paris.

Ratti, silk print from the 1994 collection. Ratti archives, Como.

this local industry ranks first worldwide in the field, a position due to the area's unique access to a network of specialists that includes designers, Jacquard-card readers, dyers, trimmers, and custom weavers, all of whom live and work in the region. The sum of their collective skills has made Saint-Étienne the ribbon capital of the world, and much of the space in the local museum of art and industry is devoted to their work. On display are antique ribbon looms, a reconstructed ribbon-glazing workshop, and sample ribbon collections illustrating the wealth and diversity of an industry that supplies ribbon and trim for many purposes (furnishing braid, fancy trim, brand labels, woven menus, badges, and so on). The antique looms exhibited at the museum are regularly operated by retired weavers who produce ribbons and other woven souvenirs on them, turning the site into a truly "living museum."

Saint-Étienne is also home to the headquarters of Houles ribbon-makers, and in 1975 there were over seven hundred family-owned workshops in the town of Jonzieux and its outskirts. Today the region's past is commemorated by the Maison de la Passementerie, a former ribbon and trim workshop now managed by retired craftsmen.

The firm of Julien Faure, founded at Saint-Étienne in 1864 by Henri Faure and today located in Saint-Just-Rambert, manufactures woven labels, solid-color and Jacquard ribbons, luxury trim and braid, scarfs, and badges. Faure has successfully adapted to today's international markets, using the most advanced Jacquard looms to create over one hundred new ribbon models and 150 original designs annually. By employing computer-assisted design techniques, Faure is able to meet the diverse artistic and technical specifications of each individual client, and to produce unique pieces in a short time.

The silk museum at Charlieu, which since 1992 has been housed in the town's renovated Hôtel-Dieu, stands as tangible proof of silk's importance to this entire region. Here again, all the looms on display are in working order, and can be used to demonstrate traditional weaving techniques similar to those illustrated in the plates of Diderot's *Encyclopedia.* Modern shuttleless air- and water-jet looms are also exhibited, along with the banners of the Charlieu weavers' guild, the last still active in France. It is in this town, famous for its abbey, that the firm of Veraseta opened its doors early this century. Veraseta is known primarily for its traditional taffetas, but today it also manufactures silk velvets on which gold leaf is applied with a hot iron—the same technique as that used for gold-tooled book-bindings. Many old weaving mills still stand throughout the region, and those idled by the slump in the French textile industry have been converted into "living museums," presenting demonstrations of traditional crafts.

At Saint-Paul-en-Cornillon, near Firminy, records kept by the Teinturerie de la Paix show that fifty percent of the yarn dyed there is silk, a statistic which indicates that silk is making a comeback in the area, for use not only by trim- and ribbon-makers, but also by weavers. This firm has made a considerable effort to preserve traditional standards of craftsmanship, and is therefore able to duplicate the exact shades needed for the reproduction of antique silks in small customized lots. The Teinturerie de la Paix also dyes yarns in subtle shades for ribbon, and multicolored jaspé yarn with ripple, asymmetrical, and other effects. This range of novelty yarns provides textile designers with the means to create highly original products for both couture and furnishing fabrics. Cuinzier, a town not far from Charlieu, is home to the design studios and fabulous archives of Quenin, a firm founded by families originating in Lyon and today owned by Lelièvre (see appendix, *The Tradition of Fine Silk*).

Tours

In a previous chapter we described the important role played by Tours since the fifteenth century, and the reign of Louis XI, as a center for silk upholstery. Although today Lyon's industrial supremacy is indisputable, Tours still boasts two major silk weavers specializing in furnishing fabrics, the Trois Tours factory, and the firm of Jean Roze (see appendix).

Paris

Most of the firms described above have offices in Paris. The French furnishing fabric syndical chamber has its headquarters in a small town house across from the Tassinari et Chatel offices, where it displays the products of its members, most of whom are silk weavers. The Perrin group, which includes a number of furnishing fabric weavers based in Lyon and Switzerland, maintains a showroom on the Place de Furstemberg. Paris also boasts its own trim- and ribbon-makers, such as La Passementerie Nouvelle (see appendix).

SILK WORLDWIDE

All of the countries with historical links to the silk trade—China, Japan, India, and Thailand in Asia; Italy and Spain in Western Europe—continue to produce magnificent silks today. India, where lost silk is still woven using traditional methods, produces fabrics of great diversity. Magnificent pure silk saris are still woven on handlooms in Varanasi (Benares) in the north of the country, and many handcrafted silks woven in other regions are exported throughout the world. Some silks which require an especially long time to weave are used only for ceremonial occasions. This is the case for the wedding saris common in the Gujarat region and known as *patola*, which means double ikat.

Japan is also a great silk producing country. Its swift adaptation to the modern industrial world has largely eliminated the traditional kimono, which provided the major outlet for local silk, and Japanese weavers are now increasingly called upon to produce fabrics suitable for western clothing styles. However, the famed Nishijin section of Kyoto, home to a venerable silk-weaving craft devoted to producing fabric for kimonos and Nō drama costumes, still boasts four thousand active hand-operated Jacquard looms for weaving opulent brocades and damasks. The Nishijin Center association, whose members include both craftsmen and industrialists, was formed to preserve textile crafts originating in sixteenth-century Ming dynasty China. In the Nakahiko workrooms, for example, *kesas* (the traditional shawls worn by Buddhist monks) are still woven.

Contemporary Italian silk production is concentrated in the northern industrial zones on the outskirts of Como and Milan. Many large Italian firms have managed to maintain the quality characteristic of antique Italian silks. Ratti-Italy, based in Como, produces woven and printed silks for fashion and furnishing. Antonio Ratti has created a foundation dedicated to preserving the ancient techniques and culture associated with Italian silk. In the furnishing sector, Lisio of Florence specializes in using hand-powered Jacquard looms for reproducing the finest antique Italian silks: ciselé velvets, damasks with complicated arabesque patterns, brocades, and lampas silks embroidered in gold and silver. For the

restoration of Italian palaces, Lisio uses old-style looms to reproduce models originally woven in the fourteenth to eighteenth centuries. The firm also uses modern power-driven Jacquard looms for weaving its contemporary furnishing-silk collections, adapting antique color ranges and designs to modern tastes.

As a strategically located trading center, Venice played a key role in the meeting between East and West, and has a long tradition of silk and velvet manufacture which continues today. The sixteenth-century Palazzo Corner Spinelli is the headquarters of Rubelli, a firm founded in 1858 in a small velvet-weaving mill located on the lagoon in the north of Venice. Rubelli has carefully preserved all its nineteenth-century archives, including the design for the San Marco scroop damask in stunning shades of gold and Veronese blue. In an appropriate tribute to the Venetian master and the colors immortalized with his name, Lorenzo Rubelli financed the restoration of Veronese's magnificent painting *Portrait of Bella Nani* in the collection of the Louvre.

The *Prix de la navette d'or* (golden shuttle award) won in 1994 by Rufelli's *Mocenigo* silk. This design is a reproduction of an extremely worn antique damask, probably from the eighteenth century. It was recreated using modern weaving techniques. The warp is natural thrown silk and the weft eighteen percent linen blended with spun rayon. The fabric's name, *Mocenigo*, is that of an old Venetian family.

In cooperation with local organizations in the Rhône-Alpes region, the French silk trade association, Inter-Soie France, has published a brochure describing all the major silk firms in the area. These include throwers, dyers, weavers, and finishers of silk for both fashion and furnishing fabrics.

FURNISHING FABRICS

Information Center

The French furnishing fabric syndical chamber has set up an information center at 36 rue Danielle-Casanova in Paris, where comprehensive information on major French furnishing fabric and trim designers and manufacturers is available. The center also offers a wide range of fabric samples available to the public for consultation, including a large selection of silk fabrics and silk trim manufactured by the principal specialists in the field. New products are added as soon as they appear in manufacturers' collections. Below we give a brief summary of the chamber's most prominent firms.

Tassinari et Chatel

Tassinari et Chatel is one of the oldest furnishing-silk manufacturers in France. The firm's archives go back to its founding in 1680 by Louis Pernon, "merchant in cloth of gold and silver." At the end of the eighteenth century, his descendant Camille Pernon hired the best designers of the day to execute the numerous commissions he received from the royal courts of Europe. As noted elsewhere in the present work, it was Pernon who wove the magnificent silk designed by Philippe de Lasalle for Marie-Antoinette. The Grand brothers, who headed the firm from 1811 to 1866, were named purveyors to the royal and imperial household. The firm passed to Messrs. Tassinari and Chatel in 1871. Since then, members of the two families have carefully preserved all the archives belonging to their prestigious firm, and today the royal courts of Europe still call on Tassinari et Chatel when fabrics are required for the restoration of their palaces. Exact reproductions of antique silks (lampas, damasks, brocades) are executed on hand-powered Jacquard looms fitted with original nineteenth-century mechanisms. Tassinari et Chatel has supplied fabrics for the restoration of Versailles, and a reproduction to replace a very worn Genoa velvet in the Prado, Madrid. In addition to reproductions of precious eighteenth- and nineteenth-century fabrics, the firm has executed contemporary designs by artist-designers such as Lalique, Majorelle, and Follot. Today, the firm of Chotard is also managed by Tassinari et Chatel.

Prelle

This firm was founded in 1749. On 30 January 1765, François Verzier, from whom Prelle's current owners are directly descended, received a letter of patent naming him "manufacturer and merchant of cloth of gold, silver, and silk in this city of Lyon." Verzier and his successors consistently worked with the best designers of their time. In the eighteenth century, one of these was Jean-François Bony, a follower of Philippe de Lasalle's

who designed large brocaded fabrics for ceremonial furnishings in royal residences. An outstanding example is the "queen's great brocade," a *gros de Tours* brocaded in a pattern of tulip and poppy bouquets decorated with peacock feathers and ribbons. Two centuries later, François Verzier's descendants Philippe and François (the sixth generation of the Verzier family) headed the firm until 1993, and today François's son Guillaume continues the tradition.

The archives belonging to this distinguished firm contain every pattern it has used over the two centuries of its existence. The firm owes its name to a remarkable nineteenth-century designer, Eugène Prelle, who worked closely with artists of the period such as Viollet-le-Duc and Charles Garnier. A Prelle brocatelle silk with a pattern of musical instruments was designed by Garnier for the foyer of the Paris opera house.

Aimé Prelle led the firm during the Art Deco period, when it executed a number of original furnishing fabrics such as the 1920 lampas silk woven from a design by Lalique for the transatlantic ocean liner *Le Paris*, and the 1930 design by Raoul Dufy for the Elysée Palace. Today, in addition to its limited editions woven on handlooms, Prelle also produces less expensive damasks, lampas silks, and brocatelles by using power-operated shuttle looms and—for some silks—even more modern types of loom. The firm's annual collections are based on its historic archives yet adapted to modern taste, in particular that of contemporary designers.

Prelle has valiantly survived all the crises that have affected the textile industry over the years. As Philippe Verzier noted in 1986: "Silk may be costly and fragile, but it is returning in force. Its intrinsic qualities are appreciated more than ever before, and a new consumer market is developing for silk furnishing fabrics." Verzier was correct in recognizing that the intrinsic characteristics of silk have a unique appeal, but these exceptional properties have been difficult to preserve. Like Tassinari et Chatel, Prelle maintains a workshop containing hand-powered Jacquard looms for weaving reproductions of the fabrics that form part of the French artistic heritage. Prelle wove the reproductions for the queen's bedchamber at Versailles, and also for the bedchamber of Louis XIV—a brocade measuring a total of 4 by 1.25 yards woven at a rhythm of just a little over one inch per day. For some of the more complicated brocades, it sometimes takes an entire day to weave just half an inch of fabric.

For the restoration of Louis XV's fabulous opera house, Prelle reproduced the silk velvet for seats in the royal box, an exquisite sky-blue moire, and a delicate floss silk. These were followed by the brocaded lampas silks for the queens' bedchamber at Fontainebleau, and numerous fabrics for restored castles located throughout Europe. This type of project involves considerable financial investment: official commissions come at irregular intervals, but the team of skilled weavers must be trained and supported continuously.

Prelle and other distinguished firms, such as Lisio of Florence, are precious repositories of skills going back to the time when the Jacquard loom was first invented—and even, as at Pernon's

heir, Tassinari et Chatel, to the dawn of silk's history and the early draw-loom. Reproductions of the most complicated antique fabrics, such as certain gold and silver brocades, and ciselé and jardinière velvets, can only be woven on hand-powered looms. This is a problem that all the best silk weavers in Lyon and Tours are faced with today.

Quenin-Lelièvre

Another extremely active firm is Lelièvre, one of France's foremost designers and manufacturers of furnishing fabrics. In 1973 Lelièvre purchased Quenin, thus acquiring the archives of this long-established firm. From the interwar period until 1965, Quenin—along with Staron and Bianchini-Férier—was a major supplier of fine silk to Poiret and other *haute couture* houses. This firm also manufactures furnishing silks and historic reproductions for the French national heritage trust and royal courts throughout the world. Quenin-Lelièvre is a perfect example of the fusion of past and future: hand-powered looms are used for weaving fabrics no modern loom could reproduce; and automatic Jacquard looms for lowering the costs of innovative modern brocades containing as many as sixteen colors. Quenin-Lelièvre draws on the original Quenin archives for the design of contemporary furnishing silks and for copies and adaptations of antique models, both of which are marketed internationally.

Brochier

This firm was founded by Jean Brochier in 1895. Between the two World Wars, Brochier worked for major Parisian interior decorators such as Leleu, executing (among many others) the magnificent damask for the French president's private dining room at the Elysée Palace. Jacques Brochier headed the firm until it was acquired in 1993 by Ratti-Italy, who today distribute its output.

Verasta

J. Lorton started out with his own modest workshop, adding a number of cottage weavers during the 1930s. Today his firm is internationally renowned, thanks primarily to its exceptional collection of silk taffetas woven in a traditional manner, and in a range of exquisite colors.

The Trois Tours Factory (Georges Le Manach)

The Trois Tours factory, today headed by Bernard Macaire, is a fascinating "living museum" containing several working hand-powered Jacquard looms, the only type on which the most complicated antique fabrics can be woven. The firm's admirably preserved archives contain an extremely wide source of material. They include a large number of large-width (1.5 yards) brocatelles and damasks, a type for which Tours is famous, and which Le Manach is currently the only firm in the world to produce. Le Manach also weaves embroidered lampas silks, brocades, and Genoa velvets in all styles up to and through Art Deco. An fine example is the "leopard-skin" velvet still popular with contemporary interior decorators.

Although France has made considerable efforts in recent years to restore the country's artistic heritage, the Tours region has received many fewer official commissions than Lyon. Tours has received no new official commissions since the restoration of Fontainebleau. Meanwhile, many lesser châteaux have been neglected in favor of Versailles, Fontainebleau, and Compiègne. It is unfortunate that the future of historic preservation in France is far from certain, while skilled weavers in Tours are forced to rely on commissions from other countries and from a few major interior decorators. And yet, they must continue working if their precious skills—transmitted from generation to generation since the dawn of silk weaving in France—are to survive.

Jean Roze

Founded in the eighteenth century and today headed by Antoinette Roze, this firm is the oldest silk weaver in France and represents twelve unbroken generations of skilled craftsmanship. It has survived all the economic crises afflicting both Tours and Lyon over the years. In 1789, the French Revolution caused a major upheaval in the Tours silk industry, but this firm continued to receive commissions from North America for its damasks and brocatelles until 1880. Roze has traditionally specialized in the reproduction of antique silks. For Queen Victoria's Jubilee, the English court commissioned a brocade designed to be worn by the Archbishop of Canterbury for the occasion. In 1960, the English court also commissioned a multicolored Louis XIV brocaded lampas silk for Buckingham Palace. This piece, which measured almost one hundred yards in length, required an entire year of work on the part of weaver Germain Roncet.

A mere twenty years ago, several hand-operated looms were still used at Jean Roze for the manufacture of the most complicated silks, but in 1972, when the firm was forced to move out of the city to a mill in the Saint-Avertin industrial park, they were replaced by power-driven Jacquard looms. Nevertheless, the old handwoven quality has been preserved. The firm possesses remarkable archives on which it draws for the reproduction of antique fabrics commissioned by the royal courts of Europe—for example, the red and gold coverlet for the royal bedchamber at the Château de Champchevrier (16th–17th century) at Cléré-les-Pins. In 1986, Antoinette Roze took over the firm from her father and, while continuing to produce traditional fabrics, she has added contemporary patterns to the firm's repertory for a collection designed by Jean-Michel Wilmotte.

Leclercq-Leroux

Although the firm of Leclercq-Leroux is located in the north of France, far from the traditional Lyon-Tours silk-weaving region, it has been manufacturing figured silks in all styles since the beginning of the nineteenth century. Today Leclercq-Leroux produces its silks on wide, computerized Jacquard looms that considerably reduce the cost of weaving complicated brocades. On view in a showroom at the firm's Paris office is a collection containing samples of the thousands of furnishing fabrics woven by Leclercq-Leroux since its foundation. Not all are made of silk, but all are woven from natural yarns such as linen, wool, and cotton, using the most intricate techniques (linen velvet, damask, figured weaves, etc.). The firm has recently added a collection of contemporary designs to its repertory of antique reproductions and adaptations.

TRIM

Reymondon

The firm of Reymondon was founded in 1870 by Duchesne, a Lyon weaver specializing in trim. In 1900, the firm was sold by Duchesne to Chalet, and in 1919 it passed to J. Reymondon, who expanded its operations. Today the firm boasts several production units located between the Saône and Loire rivers. Reymondon serves a worldwide market for all types of furnishing trim: fringe, single and double tassels, braid, and rosettes, cord, upholstery binding, and so on. All the designs in the firm's substantial archives can be reproduced on Jacquard looms. Reymondon also controls Poirier, a prominent name in the manufacture of furnishing fabrics during the interwar period.

Houles

The lineage of the Houles family goes back to an eighteenth-century wool importer in Mazamet who worked for the French royal household. Today Houles is the leading European manufacturer of both luxury and mass-market furnishing trim, and new designs by Suzanne Houles are presented throughout the world. The firm recently purchased the fabulous collection belonging to Bassereau, the last of the great trim-makers headquartered in Tours.

La Passementerie Nouvelle

Founded in 1818 by the Declercq family, La Passementerie Nouvelle has remained in the same hands ever since. The firm relies on traditional craftsmanship for reproducing antique fabrics commissioned for historic monuments, and also for its many contemporary designs. La Passementerie Nouvelle recently acquired trim-manufacturer Gomond, and is now the leading name in this sector. Archives dating from the ancien régime to the present day are in an admirable state of preservation, as is the Boudin collection. Claude Declercq and his son Jérôme continue to respect the ancient traditions of the French trim-making craft and frequently receive commissions for historic reproductions from today's foremost interior decorators.

Mention should also be made of Les Passementiers de l'Île-de-France, headed by Marie-Claude and Robert Oberti. Their manufacturing plant is located in Belloy-en-France, north of Paris. This firm offers luxurious quality collections based on antique models held in its extensive archives.

HAUTE COUTURE

Bianchini-Férier

Bianchini-Férier has been supplying fine silk to the leading Parisian and international *haute couture* houses for over a century. The firm has kept pace with changing fashions, calling on the services of major artists—such as Sonia Delaunay in the 1920s, and later Raoul Dufy—for the execution of over four thousand designs and sketches. As a result, Bianchini-Férier current designers have at their disposal archives containing over six hundred thousand textile samples and forty thousand designs that together constitute an impressive textile museum. The firm presents two new collections annually, a policy which enables it to adapt quickly to the whims of changing fashion. The firm's attitude to its craft could be summed up in the statement, "Silk is not just a material, it is a philosophy; the silk weaver places prime importance on the fabric's structure, its 'handle'"—an attitude shared by all true silk specialists. One of Bianchini-Férier's outstanding 1995 designs was a splendid white silk velvet for evening coats. The firm sponsors young designers in order to encourage contemporary textile design and discover new talent.

Bucol

Founded over two centuries ago, Bucol's archives contain over fifteen thousand designs. This wealth of documentation has enabled the firm to adapt continuously to new trends in feminine fashion. The concept of luxury associated with silk is intimately linked with the sensation of tactile pleasure the material affords through direct contact and movement. This explains the emphasis Bucol places on fabric finishing. Bucol also has a furnishing-fabrics department that works in close cooperation with furniture manufacturers. In 1988, Bucol joined the Porcher Textile group, thus gaining access to competitive facilities covering the entire production cycle, including an ultra-modern mill with the latest in high-tech equipment.

Beaux-Valette

Beaux-Valette provides a perfect example of the adventurous spirit that has consistently characterized the Silk Road. Ancestor M. Valette, born into a Lyon family that had been in the silk business since the eighteenth century, made an expedition to Peking in 1880. His son settled in Milan in 1902, but in 1930 returned to his native Lyon, where he founded the firm of Beaux-Valette. Supported by this valuable family tradition, the firm has been able to preserve the creative spirit associated with the Silk Road. The Beaux-Valette design studio can respond swiftly to the most unpredictable shifts in fashion. The firm presents two collections annually in which the major emphasis is on silk, including plaid taffetas, crepe de chine, heavy-weave velvets, and warp prints. No challenge is too great for the technical team of this energetic firm, whose sales representatives are sent around the world for six months of every year. In 1994, the firm worked closely with the world's most eminent couturiers, from Yves Saint-Laurent to Valentino, and earned ninety percent of its revenues on the export market. In order to remain as competitive as possible, Beaux-Valette works with the textile companies of the Rhône-Alpes region, calling on the very best weavers and finishers located in the area.

Guillaud

Founded early this century at Charlieu, Guillaud draws on all the skills of this region's textile industry, using both old-fashioned shuttle looms and modern automatic rapier looms. Guillaud is a major name in the natural silk sector, supplying sophisticated fabrics to *haute couture* houses, and more affordable types to the luxury ready-to-wear market. Guillaud is capable of executing the most fanciful ideas dreamt up by prestigious clients such as Chanel, Dior, Lanvin, Hermès, and other major houses worldwide. Its products feature yarn-dyed fabrics that can be woven in an infinite variety of ways, from heavy rustling taffetas to delicate duchesse satins. Thanks to a skillful combination of traditional craftsmanship and modern design, Guillaud earns over sixty percent of its revenues on the export market, proof that it is possible to keep abreast of international competition by combining the finest quality with high productivity.

Cattin

Ever since its foundation in 1926 by M. Cattin, this firm, located in the Nord-Dauphiné region, has concentrated on the design of highly original silks for *haute couture* and has worked with prestigious houses such as Dior, Saint-Laurent, Hermès, and Karl Lagerfeld. Today the family firm has adapted to revolutionary developments in weaving technology and owns over forty digital shuttleless looms, machinery which nonetheless requires traditional skills when it comes to weaving solid-color and Jacquard silks. As André Sigfied notes, "The silk industry draws continuously on a wellspring of fine craftsmanship."

It would unfortunately be impossible for us to list here all the other firms that specialize in producing innovative luxury fabrics for *haute couture*. Many have disappeared or been taken over by large corporations; others have been able to maintain their independence while adapting to new markets. One of the latter is Abraham, which in 1995 produced basket-weave silks for Saint-Laurent; others include Léonard, which produces intricately designed silk jerseys by Daniel Tribouillard, who studied the secrets of kimono patterns in Kyoto; Pétillaud, with its famed silk taffetas; and Buche, with its silk chiffons, crepes, and organzas.

SCARFS AND ACCESSORIES

A particularly interesting series of printed silk scarfs based on designs by contemporary artists was sponsored by the Galerie Maeght and produced by Bucol. Painters responsible for the limited editions include Jean Bazaine, Pol Bury, Paul Rebeyrolle, Hans Hartung, Agam, and Antoni Tapiès. A number of firms are also particularly noted for their designer silk scarfs and fashion accessories such as stoles, shawls, pocket handkerchiefs, neckties, and umbrellas.

Hermès

A special place of honor must be reserved for the famed silk scarfs which, along with the equally famous Kelly handbag, epitomize the Hermès image. The Hermès archives contain over two thousand scarf designs. Vast amounts of time have been spent by many, many people—all of them artists—on research and design for Hermès scarfs. Infinite, painstaking labor for a mere square yard of pure silk! The first step in this meticulous process is selection of a theme from Hermès the saddler's classic repertory: horses, hunting scenes, travel, or flora and fauna. The second is deciding on fade-proof color combinations chosen from a range of over two thousand shades. Third comes the choice of fabric type; and fourth, the printing method. Hermès uses the *Lyonnaise* or silk-screen method, requiring a separate frame for each one of up to forty separate colors. The final step is finishing—applying the treatment that gives Hermès scarfs their incomparable and inimitable "handle." Hermès has worked for the past twenty-five years with Perrin, one of the major textile corporations in the Rhône-Alpes region. Perrin offers the complete production cycle from throwing to weaving, and employs the most sophisticated technology at every phase in the manufacture of scarfs, neckties, swimwear, and so on. In addition to clothing and accessories, Perrin also produces luxury furnishing fabrics.

Malfroy-Million

This family firm, which has been making scarfs since 1939, sold over one million of them in 1991 worldwide, particularly in the Far East. This statistic is proof of the firm's vitality and creativity, and its responsiveness to new fashion trends for production of a diverse range of products including silk head scarfs, ascots, pocket handkerchiefs, and shawls. Malfroy-Million has also adopted the hospitable practice of opening its doors every Thursday to the public (Villa Mercedes, Saint-Genis-Laval).

BIBLIOGRAPHY

ALBRECHT-MATHEY, Elisabeth. *The Fabrics of Mulhouse and Alsace: 1750–1850.* Leigh-on-Sea, 1968.

ALGOUD, Henri. *La Soie: art et histoire.* Lyon, 1986.

ANQUETIL, Jacques. *Routes de la soie.* Paris, 1992.

BARBER, E. *Prehistoric Textiles.* Princeton, 1991.

BARNETT, June. *A Small Dictionary of Textile Terms.* New York, 1987.

BECKER, J. with the collaboration of D. B. Wagner. *Pattern and Loom: A Practical Study of the Development of Weaving Techniques in China, Western Asia and Europe.* Copenhagen, 1987.

BONNEVILLE, Françoise de. *The Book of Fine Linen.* Translated by Deke Dusinbere. Paris, New York, 1994.

BRÉDIF, Josette. *Toiles de Jouy: Classic Printed Textiles from France, 1769–1843.* London, 1989.

BROSSARD, I. *Technologie des textiles.* Paris, 1988.

BRUNELLO, F. *The Art of Dyeing in the History of Mankind.* Vincenza, 1973.

CALASIBETTA, Charlotte. *Fairchild's Dictionary of Fashion.* New York, 1988.

CARLANO, Marianne, and Larry Salmon, eds. *French Textiles from the Middle Ages through the Second Empire.* Hartford, CT 1985.

CLOUZOT, Henri, and Francis Morris. *Painted and Printed Fabrics: The History of the Manufactory at Jouy and Other Ateliers in France, 1760–1815.* New Haven, CT (Metropolitan Museum of Art Reprint), 1974.

CLOUZOT, Henri. *Le Métier de la soie en France 1466–1815.* Paris, before 1925.

CLUNAS, C., ed. *Chinese Export Art and Design.* London, 1987.

DAMASE, Jacques. *Sonia Delaunay: Fashion and Fabrics.* New York, 1991.

DEMORNEX, Jacqueline. *Madeleine Vionnet.* New York, 1991.

DE MARLY, Diana. *Christian Dior.* New York, 1990.

EMERY, I. *The Primary Structure of Fabrics.* Washington D.C., 1966.

Encyclopedia of Textiles (3rd ed.), by the editors of American Fabrics and Fashion Magazine. Englewood Cliffs, NJ 1980.

FALKE, O. *Decorative Silks.* New York, 1922.

FELTWELL, Dr. J. *The Story of Silk.* Great Britain, 1990.

FERRIER, R. W., ed. *The Arts of Persia.* New Haven, CT 1989.

FRANK, I. M., and D. M. Brownstone. *The Silk Road.* Oxford, 1986.

GEIJER, A. *A History of Textile Art.* London, 1979.

GIROUD, Françoise. *Dior.* London, 1987.

HANYO, G. *Soieries de Chine.* Paris, 1987.

HARRIS, Jennifer, ed. *5000 Years of Textiles.* London, 1993.

HECHT, A. *The Art of the Loom: Weaving, Spinning and Dyeing across the World.* London, 1989.

KENNEDY, A. *Japanese Costume.* Paris, 1990.

LAUMANN, Maryta M. *The Secret of Excellence in Ancient Chinese Silks.* Pasadena, 1984.

LI, Lillian. *China's Silk Trade: Traditional Industry in the Modern World.* Cambridge, MA, 1981.

LOPEZ, R. S. *The Silk Industry in the Byzantine Empire.* Cambridge, MA, 1945.

LYLE, D. S. *Modern Textiles.* New York, 1976.

MEZIL, Éric, and Jean Forneris. *Raoul Dufy, la passion des tissus.* Paris, 1983.

MILLER, Lesley. *Cristóbal Balenciaga.* New York, 1994.

MILLER-LEWIS, S. Jill. *Silk: The Luxurious Fabric.* Detroit, 1987.

NANAVATY, Mahesh. *Silk Production, Processing and Marketing.* Columbia, 1990.

OSMA, G. de Fortuny. *Mariano Fortuny: His Life and Work.* London, 1980.

RAU, Pip. *Ikats: Woven Silks from Central Asia.* Cambridge, MA, 1988.

ROTHSTEIN, N. *Silk Designs of the Eighteenth Century. From the Collection of the Victoria and Albert Museum.* London, 1990.

SCHOESER, Mary, and Kathleen Dejardin. *French Textiles from 1760 to the Present.* London, 1991.

SCHWARTZ, Paul R., and R. Micheaux. *A Century of French Fabrics: 1850–1950.* Leigh-on-Sea, 1964.

SCOTT, Philippa. *The Book of Silk.* New York, 1993.

STOREY, Joyce. *The Thames and Hudson Manual of Dyes and Fabrics.* London, 1992.

STOREY, Joyce. *The Thames and Hudson Manual of Textile Printing.* London, 1992.

THORNTON, Peter. *Authentic Decor.* London, 1984.

THORNTON, Peter. *Baroque and Rococo Silks.* London, 1965.

VOLKER, Angela. *Textiles of the Wiener Werkstätte, 1910–1932.* New York, London, 1994.

WHITE, Palmer. *Elsa Schiaparelli: Empress of Paris Fashion.* New York, 1995.

WILSON, K. *A History of Textiles.* 1974.

EXHIBITION CATALOGUES

Exposition de la soie, de ses applications et de son décor. Musée Galliera. Paris, 1906.

Les Folles Années de la soie. Musée Historique des Tissus. Lyon, 1975.

Fortuny. Musée Historique des Tissus. Lyon, 1980.

Soieries de Lyon. Commandes impériales. Collections du Mobilier national. Musée Historique des Tissus. Lyon, 1982–83.

Robes du soir. Musée de la Mode et du Costume. Paris, 1984.

Hommage à Christian Dior, 1947–1957. Musée des Arts de la Mode. Paris, 1984.

Hommage à Elsa Schiaparelli. Musée de la Mode et du Costume. Paris, 1984.

Soieries de Lyon. Commandes royales au XVIIIe siècle (1730–1800). Musée Historique des Tissus. Lyon, 1988–89.

The Opulent Era: Fashions of Worth, Doucet, Pingat. Brooklyn Museum. New York, 1989–90.

Femmes fin-de-siècle. Musée de la Mode et du Costume. Paris, 1990.

L'Art de la couture. Madeleine Vionnet, 1876–1975. Centre de la Vieille-Charité. Marseille, 1991.

Au paradis des dames. Nouveautés, modes et confections. Musée de la Mode et du Costume. Paris, 1993.

Madame Grès. Metropolitan Museum of Art. New York, 1994.

Le Dessin sous toutes ses coutures. Croquis, illustrations, modèles, 1760–1994. Musée de la Mode et du Costume. Paris, 1995.

TRANSLATIONS CITED

BACHELARD, Gaston. *The Poetics of Reverie.* Translated by Daniel Russell. Boston, 1969.

GLOSSARY

Antique Satin: A fabric (used primarily for furnishing) made to resemble the silk satin of earlier centuries.

Bombyx mori: The most common domesticated silkworm, which feeds on mulberry leaves.

Brocade: A figured silk or velvet fabric with gold or silver woven into it to create a raised design. *See* Brocatelle, Damask, Jacquard, Lamé

Brocatelle: A figured fabric similar to brocade, with a silk and gold weft on linen warp giving the pattern a high relief. See Brocade, Damask, Jacquard, Lamé

Canut: Popular term for the silk weavers of Lyon, derived from the name of the machines they used for cutting velvet pile.

Card-Reader: The technician responsible for arranging the pattern cards on a Jacquard loom.

Chenille (from the French *chenille*, hairy caterpillar): A tufted, velvety yarn, and fabrics woven from this type of yarn.

Chiné à la Branche: A resist-dyeing process derived from the ikat technique. The characteristic "cloud" effect is produced by warp-printing.

Chinoiserie: An ornate style of decoration based on chinoiserie motifs, especially common in eighteenth-century Europe.

Ciselé Velvet: A velvet for which some parts of the pattern are left looped and other parts cut to achieve a contrasting design.

Crepe: A lightweight fabric with a crinkled surface.

Crinoline: A smooth, stiff, strong material made of cotton warp and horsehair filling.

Damask (from *Damascus*, the city): A durable, lustrous, reversible figured fabric of silk or linen. *See* Brocade, Brocatelle, Jacquard, Lamé

Draw-Loom: A hand-operated loom, developed from an early Egyptian model and perfected by the Sassanians, on which patterns can be reproduced mechanically, hence as often as wished, once the original repeat unit has been set up by the weaver.

Duchesse: A lustrous, smooth silk made with a dense warp.

Embroidered Silk: Silk fabric for which the pattern or decoration is applied to the surface by needlework. *See* Figured Silk, Plain Silk

Fiber: An individual strand.

Figured Silk: Silk fabric for which the pattern or decoration is an integral part of the weave. *See* Embroidered Silk, Plain Silk

Filament: An individual strand of indefinite length, with a finer diameter than a fiber.

Float: A thread that is brought to the surface of a fabric in weaving, especially to form a pattern.

Floss Silk: Raw, untwisted (unthrown) silk thread reeled from the filament of the silkworm cocoon. Floss silk is generally too fragile to be woven and is used primarily as embroidery thread. *See* Silk Throwing

Gazar: A sheer silk fabric with a rustic "gauzy" look.

Gimp: a ribbon-like worsted silk, sometimes stiffened with wire.

Gros de Tours: A strong, heavy taffeta with a double weft and an interesting raised-surface texture.

Hand, Handle: The reaction of the sense of touch when fabrics are held in the hand.

Ikat (from the Turkish *abr*, cloud): A warp and/or weft resist-dyeing process used to produce a variety of linear, curved, or geometric "cloud" patterns.

Jacquard: A figured fabric woven on a Jacquard loom. *See* Brocade, Brocatelle, Damask, Lamé

Jacquard Loom: A loom invented in France by Joseph Marie Jacquard in 1804, using an endless belt of pattern cards punched with holes arranged so as to produce a figured weave. The Jacquard loom replaced the human string-pullers who manipulated the old draw-looms, thus revolutionizing the textile industry. Jacquard looms are used for weaving figured fabrics such as brocade, brocatelle, jacquard, and lamé.

Jaspé: Term applied to fabrics woven with multicolored threads or different shadings of the same color in order to give a shadow effect.

Kesa: A priestly garment made up of square patches sewn into a large, flat rectangle and supposed to resemble the rice fields once observed by the Buddha.

Kesi: Chinese tapestry-woven silks depicting naturalistic themes from Buddhist and Taoist tales.

Lace Silk: silk woven in such as way as to resemble lace.

Lamé: A figured fabric interwoven with metal threads, e.g. of gold or silver, to form a pattern. *See* Brocade, Brocatelle, Damask, Jacquard

Lampas also *Diasprum:* A figured fabric with a supplementary pattern weft woven over the main warp and ground weft weave.

Linters: Short cotton fibers adhering to the seed after the first ginning and used as cellulose filling in the manufacture of cheap blended silks.

Marocain: A ribbed crepe fabric.

Moire (n.), *Moiré* (adj.): Term applied to fabric that is folded double and pressed in a cylinder so that some ribs of the weave are flattened while others remain unflattened. The resulting contrast in the way different parts of the fabric reflect light produces a "watered" effect, and moire is also sometimes referred to as "watered silk."

Ottoman: Silk fabric with a broad, flat rib.

Paisley: A worsted fabric with a an all-over scroll design originating in Paisley, Scotland.

Panne: A soft cloth resembling velvet, but with a longer nap and a lustrous finish.

Pebrine: A disease of the silkworm that virtually destroyed the European silk industry during the mid-nineteenth century, but was eventually curbed through a process of scientific silkworm selection developed by Louis Pasteur.

Pekin: A striped silk fabric, originally from China.

Piece-Dyed: A term referring to fabrics that are dyed after they have been woven.

Plain Silk: Silk woven with no integral pattern or decoration. See Figured Silk, Embroidered Silk

Pongee: A soft, thin Chinese or Indian silk, usually a natural light brown color.

Poplin: A fabric woven with a wool weft and silk warp, or with wool, linen or cotton weft and silk warp. The name derives from the French *pape* (pope*)* and *lin* (linen*)*, since this fabric was originally made in Avignon, the city of the popes.

Resist-Dyeing: Any dyeing process in which certain parts of the fabric are coated or blocked with a substance that will not absorb the dye, thus creating a pattern.

Samite: A type of plain or figured silk. Both sides of the fabric are covered by weft floats bound in a 1:2 twill, while the main warps are concealed inside the material.

Sateen: A fabric woven as for silk and/or rayon, but made from cotton.

Satin: A term applied to fabrics woven from silk or rayon.

Screen Printing: A process in which a fine-mesh screen (formerly silk, now often a synthetic fabric) is used to apply a stencil-print to fabric.

Sericin: A resinous, amorphous gum that bonds the two gossamer filaments spun by the silkworm together, providing them with a protective coating throughout the fabric manufacturing process.

Sericulture: The rearing of silkworms.

Shantung: A fabric with a slub (nubby) filling, made from the silk of wild silkworms.

Shuttleless Loom: A loom for which the filling yarn (weft) is propelled by air or water rather than a shuttle. Because these looms are faster than conventional looms, they are more economical to operate.

Silk Reeling: The process of unwinding silk filament from the cocoon and onto spools.

Silk Throwing (from the Anglo-Saxon *thrawan*, to twist): A series of operations designed to strengthen raw reeled silk by twisting it to form a more substantial yarn. Most silks must be thrown (in throwing mills) before they can be woven. *See* Floss silk

Slub: Irregularities in a fabric weave creating an uneven, nubby effect.

Tapestry: An ornamental woven fabric in which the design is usually a picture illustrating a story.

Tiraz (from the Arabic *tarz*): Fabrics woven in official Persian workshops; also the name of the workshops themselves.

Tussah: Silk made from the cocoons of a wild or semi-domesticated silkworm of the same name, which often feeds on oak leaves.

Twill: A fabric woven so as to have parallel diagonal lines or ribs.

Velours Sabres: A satin fabric with a double warp, one structural and the other floating. After the fabric has been woven, every second thread-loop in the designated pattern is laboriously hand cut with a tiny instrument called a *sabre*. The resulting pile is then raised with a brush, giving a velvet effect against a satin background.

Velvet: A rich fabric with a soft, thick pile. For *pile velvet*, the loops are left uncut; for *cut velvet* the loops are cut apart.

Warp: The threads running lengthwise on a loom and crossed by the weft.

Warp-Printing: A process whereby the warp threads are printed before the fabric is woven, giving the finished fabric a blurred or mottled effect.

Weft also *Woof:* The yarns carried by the shuttle back and forth across the warp in weaving.

Yarn-Dyed: Fabrics for which the yarn has been dyed in the skein or package prior to weaving.

INDEX

ACKNOWLEDGMENTS

In conjunction with Pascale Ballesteros, Marc Walter, and Flammarion publishers, the author would like to thank the many people who have provided assistance, encouragement, and intellectual and material support for the present volume. In particular, we would like to mention the following:

Edouard Bonnefous, president of the Singer-Polignac foundation, for his keen interest in the book and the invaluable assistance provided by the foundation in research and document gathering.
Jean Leclant, lifetime secretary of the French Académie des Inscriptions et Belles Lettres, for his steadfast encouragement and help in establishing valuable contacts.
Doudou Diene, director of the UNESCO project "Integral Study of the Silk Roads: Roads of Dialogue," who has consistently supported our work.

Gustave Zumsteg, director of the firm of Abraham; Rodolfo Bevilacqua, of the Venetian firm Luigi Bevilacqua; François Verzier, managing director of Prelle of Lyon, and his assistant Marie-France du Bellay; Messrs. Bernay and Perrin from the Quenin firm in Cuinzier, near Charlieu; Mlle. Roze, of Jean Roze in Tours; Patrik Lelièvre of Lelièvre in Paris; Raphaël Tassinari of Tassinari et Chatel, archivist

Mme. Françoise Ducret, and Mr. Charlet of the Fontaine-sur-Saône mill; and Bernard Macaire, managing director of Trois Tours-Le Manach in Tours.

Marc Audibet, fashion designer, and Christine Blanc, press officer for Marc Audibet; Michèle Meunier and Olivier Chatenet, fashion designers for Mariot Chanet, and Danièle Pinelli, press officer for Mariot Chanet; Marika Genty, archivist for Dior; Jean-Louis Dumas, managing director of Hermès; Couturier Olivier Lapidus and Elizabeth Caron-Gendry, press officer for Olivier Lapidus; the Issey Miyake couture house and Maryvonne Numata, press officer for Issey Miyake Europe.

The curators and librarians at the various museums mentioned in the text, and in particular: Mme. Join-Dieterle, head curator, and Valérie Guillaume, curator, of the Musée de la Mode et du Costume de la Ville de Paris; the Musée Historique des Tissus, Lyon; the Musée des Arts de la Mode et du Costume, and especially Sonia Edard and Véronique Belloir; the Musée d'Art et d'Industrie in Saint-Étienne, and especially Nadine Besse; the Victoria and Albert Museum in London, and especially Joanna Wallace; the Macclesfield Museums Trust, and especially Mr. Collins and Mrs. Louanne; Mme. Denise and Mr. Amaury Lefébure,

head curator of the Musée National du Château de Fontainebleau; Jean-Marie Moulin, Conservateur en chef du Patrimoine, responsible for the Musée National du Château de Compiègne, and Mme. Maison; Mlle. Lagoutte, at the Château d'Azay-le-Rideau; Jean-Pierre Babelon, director of the Versailles and Trianon museums and national park.

Jacques Brochier, silk maker and professor at the Institut Textile et Chimique de France; Maria Giovanna Cosentino, at the Venetian firm Rubelli; Ronald Currie, secretary general of the International Silk Association; Geneviève France, of Intersoie and Unitext; Suzanne Janin-Peltier; Jean-Paul Leclerc, curator; Roberta Orsi, at the Fondazione Arte della Seta Lisio in Florence; Alberto Pezzato, at the Venetian firm Lorenzo Rubelli, and Paul Bidault, president of Rubelli France; Pia Ripamonti, at the Antonio Ratti Foundation in Como; Simone Savaté, of the Fulgence collection; and textile engineer Odile Valansot.

Lastly, Christian Brandstätter and Mr. Mouriacoux (Giraudon); Alessandra Pinzani (Scala), and Valérie Courbot (Hermès), as well as the entire team that contributed to the technical and artistic production of this book: proofreaders, researchers, photoengravers, etc.

PICTURE CREDITS